Transcendence and Wittgenstein's *Tractatus*

Transcendence and Wittgenstein's *Tractatus*

MICHAEL P. HODGES

TEMPLE UNIVERSITY PRESS

Philadelphia

Temple University Press, Philadelphia 19122
Copyright © 1990 by Temple University. All rights reserved
Published 1990
Printed in the United States of America

The paper used in this publication meets the minimum
requirements of American National Standard for Information
Sciences—Permanence of Paper for Printed Library Materials,
ANSI Z39.48-1984 ♾

Library of Congress Cataloging-in-Publication Data

Hodges, Michael P.
    Transcendence and Wittgenstein's Tractatus / Michael P. Hodges.
        p. cm.
    Includes bibliographical references.
    ISBN 0-87722-692-X (alk. paper)
        1. Wittgenstein, Ludwig, 1889–1951. Tractatus logico-
philosophicus. 2. Logic, Symbolic and mathematical. 3. Languages—
Philosophy. 4. Transcendence (Philosophy). I. Title.
B3376.W563T73345   1990
    192—dc20   89-48480
                                                                        CIP

Henceforth, my dear philosophers, let us be on guard against the dangerous old conceptual fiction that posited a "pure, will-less, painless, timeless knowing subject"; let us guard against the snares of such contradictory concepts as "pure reason," "absolute spirituality," "knowledge in itself": these always demand that we should think an eye that is completely unthinkable, an eye turned in no particular direction, in which the active and interpreting forces, through which alone seeing becomes seeing something, are supposed to be lacking; these always demand of the eye an absurdity and a nonsense. There is *only* a perspective seeing, *only* a perspective "knowing" . . . .
—F. Nietzsche, *On the Genealogy of Morals*, Third Essay, section 12

CONTENTS

LIST OF ABBREVIATIONS

References to Wittgenstein's works in the text use the following abbreviations.

CV   *Culture and Value*, ed. by G. H. von Wright, trans. by P. Winch. Oxford: Blackwell, 1980.

LE   "Wittgenstein's Lecture on Ethics." *The Philosophical Review* 74 (January, 1965): 3–27.

LLW   Paul Engelmann, ed., *Letters from Ludwig Wittgenstein with a Memoir*, ed. by B. F. McGuinness, trans. by L. Furtmuller. Oxford: Blackwell, 1967.

NB   *Notebooks 1914–1916*, ed. by G. H. von Wright and G. E. M. Anscombe, trans. by G. E. M. Anscombe. Oxford: Blackwell, 1962.

OC   *On Certainty*, ed. by G. E. M. Anscombe and G. H. von Wright, trans. by D. Paul and G. E. M. Anscombe. Oxford: Blackwell, 1969.

PI   *Philosophical Investigations*, ed. by G. E. M. Anscombe and R. Rhees, trans. by G. E. M. Anscombe. Oxford: Blackwell, 1953.

PR   *Philosophical Remarks*, trans. by R. Hargreaves and R. White. Oxford: Blackwell, 1975.

RKM   *Letters to Russell, Keynes, and Moore*, ed. by G. H. von Wright. Oxford: Blackwell, 1974.

T   *Tractatus Logico-Philosophicus*, trans. by D. F. Pears and
B. F. McGuinness. London: Routledge and Kegan Paul,
1961.

PREFACE

No book is the exclusive work of a single person. In the first place, my mother nurtured in me a sense of the importance of ideas and the pleasure of the intellectual life. I am sorry that she cannot know of this fulfillment of her dreams. I have had excellent teachers both as an undergraduate at the College of William and Mary, where my interest in philosophy was first kindled, and later at the University of Virginia, where I was continually challenged. In recent years my colleagues at Vanderbilt have been sympathetic ears and careful critics. Two deserve special mention. First, John Lachs was responsible for my initial burst of philosophical energy and continues to this day to sustain that energy as a good friend, colleague, and constructive critic. Second, Charles Scott, running partner, friend, and philosopher, has taught me more philosophy than I would have thought possible.

Several generations of undergraduate and graduate students at Vanderbilt have been kind enough to take my work seriously. Again, two deserve special mention. Tom Davis has long been a friend and sensitive philosopher who seems ever able to get to the heart of my work. Glen Erickson's enthusiasm for my ideas and for philosophy in general has always been an inspiration to me, *and* he has provided me with detailed comments that have been invaluable.

Through the years friends have sustained me with their excitement for life and ideas, none more dependably than Joel and Joyce Evans. In the last two years, no one has had a greater influence for the good on the quality of my life than Penny Harrington.

Finally, my children, Catherine and Michael, have been constant sources of love and that special energy that only children can have. Each, in very different ways, has enriched my life and with that my thought. Without them I would not have written this book.

For assistance in preparing the manuscript for publication, I must thank June Cullen and Terri Kettering at Temple, Madge Rogers, who did the proofreading and prepared the index, and Stella and Judy Thompson, secretaries to the Philosophy Department at Vanderbilt, whose continual good spirits and first-rate skills made the work a joy. I would also like to thank Tom Regan, who originally suggested that I send the book to Temple.

I have breathed the contemporary philosophical air and have been much influenced by those who shape the issues of our day. There are too many to mention and in any case readers will know who they are. Of course, no one but myself is responsible for whatever errors there certainly are in this attempt to "get a grip on Wittgenstein's thought."

Wittgenstein's philosophy has been of concern to me since 1963 when, as an undergraduate senior, I was first exposed to his work. In that encounter I found a thinker impossible to grasp and the fear that my abilities to understand philosophy had come to an end. It may be that this book will confirm that fear in the minds of many, but I hope it will bring a measure of understanding to some.

Transcendence and

Wittgenstein's

Tractatus

1

INTRODUCTION

The Historical and Cultural Background

Ludwig Wittgenstein has been and continues to be one of the most enigmatic figures in twentieth-century thought. He is a man of intense and powerful philosophical reflection who wrought not one but two major transformations of the philosophical landscape with so-called logical positivism between the world wars and then "ordinary language" philosophy in the 1950s and early 1960s, yet he would not have endorsed either position. His creative influence is certainly as alive today as it was thirty years ago, as his work undergoes transformation and reinterpretation at the hands of a new generation of thinkers, including the likes of Richard Rorty and Jean-François Lyotard. During his life he exerted a powerful personal and philosophical influence on many of the major intellectuals of the first half-century including Bertrand Russell, G. E. Moore, members of the Bloomsbury group, and a whole generation of Cambridge- and Oxford-trained philosophers and many who left the academic study of philosophy precisely because of Wittgenstein's personal influence.

He was a strange and difficult man personally who, because of incredibly high standards both intellectually and morally, was often racked with self-doubt, sometimes to the point of despair and thoughts of suicide. The story of his life is filled with tantalizing bits of information. His father, an industrialist and the founder of the

Austrian steel industry, was a family tyrant. Three of his brothers committed suicide. For some, the best-known fact about Ludwig is that his surviving brother, Paul, who lost his right hand in World War I, was a pianist of real distinction for whom Ravel wrote an important one-handed piece. Wittgenstein, heir to an extensive family fortune, gave away all of his wealth, living a life of extreme simplicity. After finishing the *Tractatus* and consistent with his claim to have found "the final solution to the problems" of philosophy (*T* preface, p. 5), Wittgenstein gave up philosophy to become an elementary school teacher. In fact, at various times he was an engineer, philosopher, architect, gardener, elementary school teacher, soldier, and medical assistant. He was an extremely complex personality who resists all attempts to reduce him to some appropriate category. Much the same can be said for his philosophical views.

Various thinkers have claimed to be inspired by his work. Perhaps the best known are the so-called logical positivists of the period between the wars. In fact, the *Tractatus Logico-Philosophicus*, Wittgenstein's only work actually published in his lifetime, has until recently been read almost exclusively as the bible of positivist thinking. For the positivists, natural science provides the paradigm of meaningful assertion, and Wittgenstein certainly seems to express that view when he says, "The totality of true propositions is the whole of natural science" (*T* 4.11). If the propositions of natural science are alone true, this implies that ethical claims, religious hypotheses, aesthetic judgments—in short, anything that cannot be brought under the rubric of natural science—must be nonsense. Since what seems to be essential to a scientific claim is its capacity to be empirically verified, the positivist took verifiability as the sine qua non of all meaningful assertions. But religious claims, for example, notoriously resist that possibility, so they must be literally meaningless! Thus whole areas of human concern could be set aside as without serious content.

Now, the *Tractatus* does attempt to carefully distinguish the meaningful from the meaningless and in a way that coincides with positivism. However, what is really decisive at this juncture is the way in which the positivists are interested in the domain of meaningful assertions. For them, the *Tractatus* sets the limits to what can be said, but, and this is critical, for the sake of what can be said. The point is to distinguish the meaningful from the meaningless so as to get on with the tractable problems that fall within the domain of the meaningful, in short, to get on with the serious business of science. Whatever falls outside this circle is either a matter of confused thinking to be clarified by philosophical analysis or not a statement at all but a mere expression of emotion. This attitude is best exemplified in A. J. Ayer's dismissive treatment of ethics and religious belief in *Language, Truth, and Logic*;[1] there certainly are passages from the *Tractatus* that support it. For example, Wittgenstein says of philosophy:

> Philosophy does not result in 'philosophical propositions', but rather in the clarifications of propositions.
> Without philosophy thoughts are, as it were, cloudy and indistinct: its task is to make them clear and to give them sharp boundaries. (*T* 4.112)

However, Wittgenstein never holds the positivist view. In various places he devotes careful and sustained attention to the ethical (LE passim), to talk about God (*NB* pp. 72–74), and to the aesthetic (*T* 6.421, *NB* p. 83). In fact, I will argue that an understanding of the aesthetic is at the very center of his own account of the highest fulfillment of the will.

Paul Engelmann provides the key to a reinterpretation of Wittgenstein's early thinking by suggesting that the reading that the positivists gave to the *Tractatus* is actually a mirror image of Wittgenstein's view. He says, in a passage we will need to discuss in more detail later:

A whole generation of disciples was able to take Wittgenstein for a positivist because he has something of enormous importance in common with the positivists: he draws the line between what we can speak about and what we must be silent about just as they do. The difference is only that they have nothing to be silent about. Positivism holds—and this is its essence—that what we can speak about is all that **really matters** in life. *Whereas Wittgenstein passionately believes that all that really matters in human life is precisely what, in his view, we must be silent about.* When he nevertheless takes immense pains to delimit the unimportant, it is not the coastline of that island which he is bent on surveying with such meticulous accuracy, but the boundary of the ocean. (*LLW* p. 97)

So when Wittgenstein says, near the end of the *Tractatus*, that the solution to the riddle of life is not a matter for natural science, he is not claiming that there is no riddle, but that science is not capable of solving it.

In *Wittgenstein's Vienna* Allan Janik and Stephen Toulmin offer an explanation for the narrow reading that Wittgenstein has received. They contend that he has been misunderstood because he has been read too exclusively against the background of philosophical issues that dominated the Cambridge of Russell and Moore, leaving out the intellectual heritage of Vienna.[2] What this truncated vision allowed was a reading of the *Tractatus* in which the logical doctrines, so important to the positivists, were taken in isolation from the certainly cryptic but fascinating ethical claims in the final sections of the book. But, according to Janik and Toulmin, the *Tractatus* is an essentially ethical work, and Wittgenstein actually said as much himself. In a famous letter to von Ficker he says, referring to the *Tractatus*, "the book's point is an ethical one."[3] However, his remark has been ignored or simply downplayed in the intellectual climate that surrounded the work. Even as recent and as well known an interpreter as P. M. S. Hacker merely dismisses the comment, saying, "Wittgenstein's letter to von Ficker is either self-deluding, or disingenuous."[4] This is a very strange interpretive position. Surely Wittgenstein should be taken seriously when he tells us what his work is all about. At the very least, such a dismissal could be justified only by the failure of serious attempts to construct such an interpretation. Hacker certainly provides none. Such a sweeping rejection of Wittgenstein's own understanding of his work should make us very suspicious. But it does show just how strong the tide is, or was, in favor of the "purely logical" view of the *Tractatus*.

All this, Janik and Toulmin attempt to correct by offering a rich picture of the intellectual context that was Vienna just before the turn of the century. Specifically, they argue that the logical and ethical dimensions of the *Tractatus* are but elements in a single vision that become clear only by laying out

the cross-interactions among (1) social and political development, (2) the general aims and preoccupations in different fields of contemporary art and science, (3) Wittgenstein's personal attitude toward questions of morality and value, and (4) the problems of philosophy, as these problems were understood in the Vienna of 1900 and as Wittgenstein himself presumably conceived them when he embarked on the inquiries of which the *Tractatus* was the end product.[5]

In this light, Wittgenstein's work can be seen as the culmination of a very different tradition from that of the logical positivists. His was the project of "reconciling the physics of Hertz and Boltzmann with the ethics of Kierkegaard and Tolstoy, within a single consistent exposition."[6] The very definition of Wittgenstein's project already and essentially contained the ethical because he was not interested in physics alone but in "reconciling the physics of Hertz and Boltzmann with the ethics of Kierkegaard and Tolstoy." Thus the ethical remarks at the end of the *Tractatus* must be seen as fundamentally connected to the logical thinking.

The reference to Kierkegaard is particularly helpful because of his sense, which comes through so clearly in *Fear and Trembling*,[7] that at the highest level—the religious—it is not a matter of what one does "in the world" that is the real issue but what one's relation is to the world taken as a whole. The "trick" is to mediate one's relation to the world through an immediate and absolute relation to God. Thus, as Kierkegaard develops it, Abraham's "claim" to Issac is only that God's will be done. Oddly, as we shall see, this is also Wittgenstein's view.

If the ethical, as Wittgenstein sees it, is not concerned with how the facts of the world are arranged, then natural science—physics, among others—which includes all true propositions and thus describes all those facts and nothing else, will not be able to speak to any ethical question. Rather, the ethical question will arise just when the totality of facts is already given. "The facts all contribute only to setting the problem, not to its solution" (*T* 6.4321). In this sense the "truths of physics" set the problem and do not solve it, but, of course, that means that they cannot be incompatible with the solution either. Natural science offers a particular picture of the world while ethics deals with the meaning or value of the picture thought of as already completed.

The ethical has nothing to do with anything "in the world" but with the world taken as a whole—as God wills it. And this exactly parallels his view, on the logical side, that to see the world aright is not a matter of getting straight on any particular facts—"Philosophy is not one of the natural sciences" (*T* 4.111). Rather, it is a matter of grasping the world as the totality of facts (*T* 1.1). So, the happy person is not the one who is caught up in the affairs of the world but the one who wills the world as God wills it—from without as a given totality (*NB* p. 74, 8.7.16). Of course, this will become clearer in subsequent chapters.

Not only do Janik and Toulmin claim that the essential task of the *Tractatus* is ethical but they also argue that, for Wittgenstein, there is a very close connection between the ethical and the aesthetic. Again, we have Wittgenstein's own word on it. "Ethics and aesthetics are one and the same" (*T* 6.421), but the aesthetic cannot be understood as the merely decorative. Such a reduction involves a fundamental misunderstanding. "People nowadays think that scientists exist to instruct them, poets, musicians, etc., to give them pleasure. The idea that these [poets etc.] have something to teach them—that does not occur to them" (*CV* p. 36).[8] The idea of the aesthetic as the decorative is the view that it is the role of the poet or musician merely to give us pleasure. But this notion of decoration involves a confusion that is destructive to both the functional and the aesthetic. In the Vienna of Wittgenstein's day,

> decoration was "applied" from outside to everything from beer mugs to doorknobs. In this, Loos [an architect and formative figure of the era] perceived a mixture of fact and fantasy that was highly detrimental to both. The principles of designing objects for use should be purely factual and determined by the functions that the objects are to serve. Such artifacts ought to be as simple and serviceable as possible. Their design ought to be so "rational" that any two artisans faced with the same task would produce identical objects.[9]

Mere decoration has no place in the "purely factual" world of useful objects, and it is "detrimental" to the aesthetic—what is here called fantasy—to be conceived in this mode. It is detrimental just because it denies the possibility that "poets have something to teach us" (*CV* p. 36) and so reduces the significance of the aesthetic to the merely pleasant.

For Wittgenstein's generation, "aestheticism became the only alternative to immersion in business affairs. So art which had earlier been the decoration adorning middle-class success in business became for the younger generation an avenue of escape."[10] In a rudimentary form, the essential ethical insights of the *Tractatus* begin to take shape. Begin with a distinction between the aesthetic and the rational or factual and conceive the aesthetic as an escape from the world of reason and fact. Now if, as Wittgenstein contends in the *Tractatus*, the world of reason and fact just is the world—"the world is the totality of facts" (*T* 1.1)—there will be no place in the world for the aesthetic. To locate it in the world would be to reduce it to the merely pleasant. But since a proposition is a picture of a fact (*T* 4.1), what is adequate to express the totality of facts—language—will be inadequate to the aesthetic. Thus the aesthetic is pushed beyond the world and language.

Now we can return to Wittgenstein's cryptic remark that ethics and aesthetics are one and the same. What Wittgenstein means here is that the ethical is absorbed into an aesthetic appreciation of the world. The world—the totality of facts—is not, in its ethical meaning, a field of actions within which we move; it is an aesthetic object to be contemplated and enjoyed. In this way Wittgenstein is able to develop a vision of the ethical that exactly parallels the better known logical views.

In Wittgenstein's hands, and driven by his comprehensive critique of language, we arrive at a distinction between the expressible world of fact and the inexpressible realm of ethical-aesthetic value that lies at the limit of the world. Janik and Toulmin certainly see the importance of the aesthetic for Wittgenstein when they say that the *Tractatus* "assigns a central importance in human life to art, on the ground that art alone can express the meaning of life,"[11] but nowhere do they work out the details of such a view. Nowhere do they show just what this comes to in the context of the *Tractatus* itself. However, it is essential to do that if we are to understand Wittgenstein thoroughly, both in his earlier and later periods, and that is what I propose to do here.

There is a second, and perhaps less excusable weakness in Janik's and Toulmin's treatment. Certainly there can be no quarrel with the main lines they develop. At least, the general thrust of the argument is perfectly acceptable. Any adequate understanding of the *Tractatus* must take, as central, its ethical insights and understand the logical aspects in a way that is coherent with them. However, since the central contention of their book is that Wittgenstein scholarship has suffered because his Cambridge background has been treated in isolation from that of Vienna, it is most surprising that they continue that by treating Wittgenstein's Vienna in isolation from Cambridge. They ignore aspects of the intellectual world of Cambridge that would have reinforced and transformed the understanding of the meaning and role of the aesthetic that Wittgenstein brought with him from Vienna. In fact, there are at least four interrelated factors. The first two are G. E. Moore's own value theory and the Bloomsbury group. These are, of course, interrelated because it is well known that Moore had a great influence on that group. However, there is a third and completely overlooked influence—Edward Bullough and his essay " 'Psychical Distance' as a Factor in Art and an Aesthetic Principle," which first appeared in the *British Journal of Psychology* in 1912—the very year that Wittgenstein came to Cambridge.[12] Bullough offers an account of aesthetic experience independent of the concerns of the *Tractatus* but that, nonetheless, bears a striking similarity to the Tractarian model and that shows how the logical transcendence of the *Tractatus* is the very condition necessary for the aesthetic contemplation of the world. Finally, there is Russell's own ethical thinking in this period, especially in "A Free Man's Worship." [13] Let us begin with Moore and the Bloomsbury group.

Perhaps because of the immense attention the critical aspects of Moore's *Principia Ethica*[14] received—the critique of hedonism, the naturalistic fallacy, the indefinability of the good, and so forth—its own unique theory of intrinsic value has not been carefully studied.[15] However, that is certainly very significant for an understanding of the intellectual climate of Cambridge during this period. Janik and Toulmin stress the importance of the aesthetic for Wittgenstein's Vienna and contend that Wittgenstein has been read against the narrow logical background of Moore and Russell. But for Moore, the ethical is at least partially absorbed by the aesthetic. In fact, Moore identifies only two things that have overriding and intrinsic value. "By far the most valuable things, which we know or can imagine, are certain states of consciousness, which may be roughly described as the pleasures of human intercourse and the enjoyment of beautiful objects." [16] It is only the enjoyment of beautiful objects—along with the pleasures of human intercourse—in light of which "any one can be justified in performing any public or private duty; . . . they are the *raison d'etre* of virtue." [17] In the end, for Moore, what makes life worth living—what gives it value—is the enjoyment of others and of beautiful things. Specifically ethical goods, virtues, for example, have their value by reference to the aesthetic.

For Moore all this is set in the context of a utilitarian view that defines the right in terms of the good, and Wittgenstein would certainly have rejected all that. But what is important for us is that Moore gives such overriding value to the aesthetic—to the enjoyment of beautiful things. His placing the aesthetic at the center of the ethical life is highly suggestive and has been completely overlooked in the attempt to understand Wittgenstein's thought. But if Janik and Toulmin are correct, and I believe that they are in this regard, it would have been striking and confirming for the young Wittgenstein to find Moore giving such pride of place to the aesthetic. Wittgenstein would have seen in Moore's "aestheticism" a position that was at least "on the right track." [18]

Although Moore's discussion of intrinsic value in terms of the pleasures of human intercourse and the appreciation of beautiful things has not been at the center of philosophical discussions of *Principia Ethica*, it could be argued that those very values became the living creed of the Bloomsbury group. In the writings of Virginia Woolf, for example in *To the Lighthouse*, she focuses on the importance of the pleasures of human intercourse and aesthetic creativity and appreciation, especially over against the impersonality of "philosophical truth."[19] That the Bloomsbury group was deeply influenced by Moore's work is clear from many reports by members. J. M. Keynes said of *Principia Ethica*, "it was exciting, exhilarating, the beginning of a renaissance, the opening of a new heaven on a new earth,"[20] and Virginia Woolf "struggled through *Principia Ethica* page by page in 1908."[21] In fact, Alasdair MacIntyre has suggested that "the group who were to become Bloomsbury had already accepted the values of Moore's sixth chapter"[22] and found in it a way of grounding their acceptance in a "rational" procedure. Since the members of the Bloomsbury group were widely influential, both individually and as a group, their acceptance of the centrality of the aesthetic in a conception of the intrinsically valuable would have a deep influence on the intellectual atmosphere into which Wittgenstein entered in 1912.

I am not attempting to construct a complete argument on this matter, by any means. To do so would require a much more careful look at the whole social and cultural context that was England during the pre–World War I period, including, at a minimum, a careful assessment of the import of Oscar Wilde. My interest, however, is not intellectual history but philosophy (but I do not mean to suggest that the two are totally unrelated to each other). Nonetheless, Wittgenstein would have found in the Cambridge of his day strains of thought confirming the very elements that Janik and Toulmin identify as *essentially* Viennese and as essential to a full understanding of his early philosophy.

At the center of Wittgenstein's early position is its transcendent perspective—a perspective from which the world, the totality of facts, can appear as a totality. The entire work, its problematic and its positive claims, are essentially shaped by that. The author of the *Tractatus Logico-Philosophicus* stands beyond what is "described" in the work, but since what is described there is *the world and language,* that author must be "beyond the world and language." In a somewhat uncharacteristic passage, Wittgenstein puts the point as follows:

> If I wrote a book called *The world as I found it,* I should have to include a report on my body, and should have to say which parts were subordinate to my will, and which were not, etc., this being a method of isolating the subject, or rather of showing that in an important sense there is no subject; for it alone could *not* be mentioned in that book.—
>
> The subject does not belong to the world: rather, it is a limit of the world. (*T* 5.631–632)

I will argue that the book—*The World as I found it*—is the *Tractatus* and that the subject who wrote it must therefore be "beyond the world."

What is fascinating from a historical point of view is that this very notion of "being beyond"—of transcending—is identified by Edward Bullough in his classic essay as the essential feature of all aesthetic experience. As I noted earlier, that essay appeared in 1912, the very year that Wittgenstein came to Cambridge, where Bullough was a professor of classics. I do not mean to suggest that Wittgenstein read the article (I know of no evidence on that matter), nor that he was directly familiar with Bullough's work. Rather, my point is that such ideas were "in the air" at Cambridge and should be included in any account of the intellectual background that helped to shape Wittgenstein's ideas. What is Bullough's thesis?

In trying to identify and describe "psychic distance" as the essential aspect of aesthetic experience, Bullough says,

> It is a difference of outlook, due—if such a metaphor is permissible—to the insertion of Distance. This Distance appears to lie between our own self and its affections, using the latter term in

its broadest sense as anything which affects our being, bodily or spiritually, e.g., as sensation, perception, emotional state or idea. Usually, though not always, it amounts to the same thing to say that the Distance lies between our own self and such objects as are the source or vehicles of such affections.[23]

Clearly, what he has in mind bears a very close relation to what I have called Wittgenstein's transcendence. Psychic distance is a matter of standing outside the object perceived in the sense that it is not taken, as it normally would be, as related to our immediate practical interests. Bullough contrasts two experiences of a fog at sea. In the first we are engaged—the fog is a danger to us—and it is "an experience of acute unpleasantness,"[24] likely to arouse anxiety and fear. However, he says, if we but "abstract from the experience of the sea fog . . . its danger and practical unpleasantness,"[25] it can be a source of intense relish and enjoyment. In the latter case, we attend to the intrinsic feature of the scene before us; it becomes an aesthetic experience. Bullough goes on to describe it as a matter of "putting the phenomenon, so to speak, out of gear with our practical, actual self; by allowing it to stand outside the context of our personal needs and ends—in short, by looking at it 'objectively.' "[26]

Suppose that one were to view the whole world—Wittgenstein's "totality of facts"—in this way, not as a field of action *in* which we are immersed but as "out of gear with our practical, actual self." This "looking at it 'objectively' " when applied to the world itself implies that "the world is *given* to me, i.e. my will enters into the world completely from outside as into something that is already there" (*NB* p. 74, 8.7.16). Thus the logical transcendence that structures his theory of logic and language is transformed into an aesthetic appropriation of the world. The first is the fulfillment of the self as knower and the second is the fulfillment of the self as will—ethical fulfillment! For Wittgenstein, to see the world aright and to will it aright are one and the same.

The idea that human salvation lies in transcendence had, in fact, been a part of the Cambridge intellectual context at least from 1903, the original date of the publication of Russell's "A Free Man's Worship." In that essay and later in "The Essence of Religion," Russell was already working with some of the central ethical ideas that Wittgenstein subsequently developed.[27] For example, in the first he says,

> To abandon the struggle for private happiness, to expel all eagerness of temporary desire, to burn with passion for eternal things—this is emancipation, and this is a free man's worship. And this liberation is effected by a contemplation of Fate; for Fate itself is subdued by the mind which leaves nothing to be purged by the purifying fire of time.[28]

There are a number of ideas here that appear in more systematically developed form in Wittgenstein's Tractarian thought. First, there is the idea that the attempt to satisfy "temporary desire" is a project doomed to failure. As we shall see, this is connected with Wittgenstein's views about the will. Second, there is the claim that only by abandoning that project and burning "with passion for eternal things" can we achieve happiness. Human fulfillment consists in escaping from our merely animal aspect, which "finds it intolerable to suppose that the universe is unaware of the importance of its own desires," but "the divine part does not demand that the world shall conform to a pattern: it accepts the world, and finds in wisdom a union which demands nothing of the world. . . . Every demand is a prison, and wisdom is only free when it asks nothing.[29] Third, there is the identification of the order of things with "Fate." In the *Notebooks 1914–1916* Wittgenstein says, "We *are* in a certain sense dependent and what we are dependent on we can call God. In this sense God would simply be fate or, what is the same thing: The world—which is independent of our will." But, Wittgenstein goes on to say, "I can make myself independent of fate" (*NB* p. 74, 8.7.16). He does not explain how in this passage, but the language of "fate" and with it the suggestion that we can be free—"emancipated" in Russell's terms—is clearly reminiscent of Russell's own discussion.

There is a further and striking indication of influence. McGuinness comments that during this period (1916–1917) Russell had a "loss of faith in the objectivity of good and evil to which he drew attention in his comments" in the preface to *Mysticism and Logic*.[30] Interestingly, Wittgenstein goes on to say, in the very passage quoted above from July 8, 1916, "I am either happy or unhappy, that is all. It can be said: good or evil do not exist." That there was influence on these points is difficult to doubt, although we might wonder which way it was going at the time.

If, as Russell contends, contemplation is a means of accepting the world, then seeing the world aright—seeing it as a whole from a disinterested perspective—would not be a mere intellectual achievement. Rather, it would bring in its train the "aesthetic" contemplation and appreciation that Wittgenstein identifies.[31] In this sense the logical work that aims at situating the reader in the position of the subject—at the limit of the world, not in it—is a necessary preparation for *and an ingredient* in the latter.

This line of discussion also allows us to explain why Wittgenstein was so dissatisfied with this part of Russell's work (and with Moore's discussion of value as well). Wittgenstein believed that attempts to "say something" about matters of value always fail. Ethical matters are just the sorts of things about which we should remain silent. Language can picture the facts, but it cannot express the meaning or value of the facts. If it could, meaning would be but another fact among the totality of facts and so not meaning at all (*T* 6.41). However, that does not imply that he did not respect the attempt to speak about value—in the "Lecture on Ethics" he says of ethics that "it is a document of a tendency in the human mind which I personally cannot help respecting deeply and I would not for my life ridicule it" (LE p. 12)—nor does it imply that he disagreed with what is meant —"what the solipsist *means* is quite correct, only it cannot be *said*, but makes itself manifest" (*T* 5.62). The real problem, for Wittgenstein, is to remain silent, and that is exactly what he thought he had done in the *Tractatus*. He says, "I believe that where many others [Moore and Russell, if I am right] today are just gassing, I have managed in my book to put everything firmly into place by being silent about it."[32]

If what we have just said about the connection between seeing the world aright—contemplation—and willing it aright is correct, then it would be a matter of "just gassing" to recommend or assert the value of contemplation. One should simply do it. The value of philosophy[33] would be manifest only to one who had *already* thought through it.[34]

The point to be made here is simply that the fact that Wittgenstein expressed deep misgivings about what both Moore and Russell had to say in these areas, as he certainly did, cannot be taken to imply that he was not deeply influenced by their ideas and even in agreement with them.

Janik and Toulmin are no doubt correct when they claim that Wittgenstein's early philosophy—and by implication his later work—has been seen against too narrow a backdrop. However, to correct that fault it is not enough to develop the continental component. Again and again we see that the Cambridge environment is a good deal richer than commentators have allowed and even richer than Janik and Toulmin would have liked to admit. We must also reevaluate the England into which he came. It is my contention that Wittgenstein's Vienna and Wittgenstein's Cambridge are by no means as distant as might be supposed.

Philosophical Issues

Along with this traditional scholarly attention, a great deal of contemporary constructive philosophy, both in the Anglo-American and continental traditions, owes or claims to owe a great debt to Wittgenstein's later philosophy. Everything from his critique of Frazer's

Golden Bough to his attack on essentialism and even his under-lying political vision has been taken as the source of radical new philosophical insight. Commentators and constructive philosophers alike (and controversy surrounds the question of who is which) have claimed that Wittgenstein's work holds the key for dealing with the problem of mind, the nature and legitimacy of religious belief, and the problem of universals.

It is paradoxical that a thinker who claimed that his "real" philo-sophical discovery was one that allowed him to stop doing philoso-phy should generate so much philosophical activity (*PI* 133). Of course, Wittgenstein is not the only twentieth-century thinker to an-nounce the end of philosophy. But such announcements inevitably provoke the response that one is continuing philosophy by announc-ing its end. A number of thinkers, including most recently Richard Rorty, have announced "the end of philosophy" and have done so on Wittgenstein's authority. Although much that Rorty and others have to say is suggestive and perhaps even correct, it is not always easy to see exactly what those who make this sort of constructive use of Wittgenstein's later philosophy are rejecting. Such proclamations of the end of philosophy can be understood only if a clear specification of what it is that has come to an end can be given (and, of course, what it means to say it has "come to an end"). But where are we to look for an example of that philosophy which is supposed to have ended? In Wittgenstein's case we have a resource for answering these questions that is not usually present—the turn in Wittgenstein's own thought.

It is odd that much of the ongoing debate pays little or no atten-tion to the one resource that Wittgenstein himself said offers a seri-ous prospect of substantial help in gaining clarity—his own earlier thinking. He says,

> Four years ago I had occasion to re-read my first book (the *Tractatus Logico-Philosophicus*) and to explain its ideas to someone. It suddenly seemed to me that I should publish those

old thoughts and the new ones together: that the latter could be seen in the right light only by contrast with and against the background of my old way of thinking. (*PI* p. viii)

Wittgenstein made the philosophical turn that Rorty and others currently recommend. A clear account of the transformation in his own thought should offer an avenue to understanding much that is under debate in current philosophical circles.

Until recently, however, little or no attention has been given to understanding that turn. There are obviously two radically distinct periods in Wittgenstein's thought, but, with one or two notable exceptions, discussions tend to treat the two independently or, at best, to consider only replies and counterreplies from one direction or the other. Various writers have pointed to arguments in the *Philosophical Investigations* that clearly have as their target the "claims" of the *Tractatus*, and this is surely helpful. However, the *Philosophical Investigations* is not a piecemeal critique of specific doctrines in the *Tractatus*. Rather, it embodies a gestalt shift—a new seeing —like those discussed in the second part of the *Investigations*. Of course, the *Philosophical Investigations* contains criticisms of specific "claims" made in the *Tractatus* but, more important, it contains a radically new way of thinking that can only be "seen in the right light . . . against the background of . . . [the] old way." The transition from the *Tractatus* to the *Philosophical Investigations* should, perhaps, be compared to the sort of "conversion" that Wittgenstein describes in *On Certainty*.

May someone have telling grounds for believing that the earth has only existed for a short time, say since his own birth? Suppose he has always been told that,—would he have any good reason to doubt it? . . . [w]hy should not a king be brought up in the belief that the world began with him? And if [G. E.] Moore and this king were to meet and discuss, could Moore really prove his belief to be the right one? I do not say that Moore could not convert the king to his view, but it would be a conversion of a special kind; the king would be brought to look at the world in a different way. (OC 92)

The later Wittgenstein plays the role he assigns to G. E. Moore in this passage. The task of the *Investigations* is to convert us, to get us to see the concerns of the *Tractatus* in "a different way." Arguments will not have any power until we do.

What, then, is the nature of the transformation that caused the Wittgenstein who thought that the *Tractatus* was "unassailable and definitive" (T preface, p. 5) to utterly repudiate his earlier work? To clarify that transformation, I will offer an interpretation of the *Tractatus* that focuses on a single idea—transcendence. With that notion, the project and doctrines of the *Tractatus* are intelligible, but once it is abandoned, the early work almost literally turns "inside out" to become the later philosophy. The account of the *Tractatus* offered here is for the sake of the later philosophy. My interest in the *Tractatus* is exactly that expressed by Wittgenstein in the passage cited from the preface to the *Philosophical Investigations*. It is in order to see the later philosophy in the "right light" that this analysis has been undertaken. At the same time, I am committed to seeing the *Tractatus* through by clearly discerning its animating principle: transcendence.

Wittgenstein's philosophical work, both early and late, centers on language, not as one among a variety of philosophical problems, but as the very subject matter of philosophy. But the problem of language in the *Tractatus* presupposes the possibility of grasping language and the world from the "outside" so that each appears as a "limited whole," and this is what I mean by "transcendence." The perspective from which the *Tractatus* is written is that of what Wittgenstein calls the "metaphysical subject" of 5.6 to 5.641 which "does not belong to the world: rather it is a limit of the world" (T 5.632). The very term "language" in the *Tractatus* reflects the issue here. On the one hand, it refers to an item in the world—one aspect of the totality of facts that is the world and that is essential to the whole picture theory of language. Only if a proposition is itself a fact can it share logical form with the fact it represents. So, Wittgenstein says, "A picture [a proposition] is a fact" (*T* 2.141). On the other hand, language is that which represents the world—the totality of facts—and since representation necessarily takes place from a position outside what is represented (see *T* 2.173), language, taken as a whole, is itself transcendent since it must be "outside" the world that it represents, even including the facts that are language itself. The "subject" required to carry out the project of the *Tractatus*—the perspective from which the work is written—is a subject essentially "outside" what it describes, which, in the case of the *Tractatus*, is both language and the world.

The doctrine of the metaphysical subject developed in 5.6 to 5.641 is in no way isolated. In fact, in the opening sentences of the *Tractatus* the "perspective of the metaphysical subject" is presupposed. Consider:

> The world is *all* that is the case.
> The world is the *totality* of facts, not of things. (*T* 1, 1.1, my emphasis)

From the beginning he speaks from the outside of the world as a whole—as a totality—given complete. Such a vision cannot be achieved if one begins in the midst of things. From there, there is no determinate "totality." There are merely indeterminate horizons that are not fixed but that are constantly changing to allow new possibilities to appear and disappear. The task of the *Tractatus*, setting the logical limits of language, requires that we transcend both language and the world, grasping each as a "limited whole."

Suppose, however, that the world cannot be grasped as a totality. Suppose that each perspective is itself an item in the world, one among a variety of possible perspectives, itself situated in relation to others. On these terms, the "project of the *Tractatus*" cannot even be intelligibly proposed. Instead of the Tractarian image of language as a phenomenon possessing essential unity, the "absolute limits" of which we can seek to articulate, there will be a multiplicity of "language-games," each with its own rules and limits. And even this multiplicity will not be something that can be grasped as a totality once and for all.[35]

We can now present the great paradox of the *Tractatus*. The perspective that is absolutely essential to the task of the work is one about which and from which we must remain silent. The propositions of the *Tractatus* "serve as elucidations in the following way: anyone who understands me eventually recognizes them as nonsensical" (*T* 6.34). Apparently, the book called *The World as I found it* is nonsensical, and that book is the *Tractatus* itself. Wittgenstein ends his work with the claim: "What we cannot speak about we must pass over in silence" (*T* 7). This would seem to imply that the *Tractatus* should not have been written. What it "says" should have been "passed over in silence."

Wittgenstein thought that the paradox arises only in relation to the problem of thought and the world, and not to that of language and the world. As he says in the preface of the *Tractatus*:

> The aim of the book is to set a limit to thought, or rather—not to thought, but to the expression of thoughts: for in order to be able to set a limit to thought, we should have to find both sides of the limit thinkable (i.e. we should have to be able to think what cannot be thought).
>
> It will therefore only be in language that the limit can be set and what lies on the other side of the limit will simply be nonsense. (*T* p. 3)

However, even as reformulated, the task is strictly an impossible one.

If we begin by giving primacy to language and its structure, it becomes at one and the same time necessary and essentially impossible to articulate the relation between the structure of "real things" and the structure of language. The difficulty rests with the limits of what can be said. Once we have separated language from the world and raised the question about the meaningfulness of language as such, nothing that can be said or thought—for, of course, what can be thought can be said—can properly be seen as an answer.

What would be needed to solve the problem is some non–language-bound *statement* of the relation between language and the world. Wittgenstein recognized this even before the doctrines of the *Tractatus* had taken final form. In the *Notebooks* we find an entry dated March 11, 1914: "What can be said can only be said by means of propositions, and so nothing that is necessary for the understanding of *all* propositions can be said" (*NB* p. 25). But the *Tractatus* does attempt to set out what "is necessary for the understanding of *all* propositions." It seems to follow that "what lies on the other side of the limit" cannot *simply* be nonsense. The propositions of the *Tractatus*, in order to accomplish their purpose, must be a language that is not language! They must give linguistic expression to what cannot be said. And this is exactly what Wittgenstein thought they did.

The "transcendental point of view" is, of course, explicitly rejected in the doctrines of the *Tractatus*, so the positions expressed in it stand in dramatic conflict with the perspective the work takes. There can be no resolution of this conflict within the philosophical framework of the *Tractatus*. Wittgenstein's famous distinction between what is said by a sentence and what that sentence shows is designed, at least in part, to overcome the difficulty. Even if we cannot "say" what the *Tractatus* seems to express, language nonetheless shows it. If we will pay attention not to what is asserted or denied, that is, to what facts are "said" to obtain, but rather to what is displayed in the very saying itself, the doctrines of the *Tractatus* will become accessible. Unfortunately, that distinction does not solve the problem; it merely gives it a name. If we ought to attend to what language shows and remain silent, what are the "propositions" of the *Tractatus* supposed to do? Do they attempt to "say" what language "shows?" But "what *can* be shown, *cannot* be said" (*T* 4.1212).

This is not to suggest that the *Tractatus* is in any sense slipshod or sloppy. Nothing could be further from the truth. It is a masterwork of philosophy, incredibly brief (eighty pages of numbered propositions, and less than half that if arranged in a continuous text), containing systematic and penetrating thought on a full range of philosophical issues. It is a work that is so tightly constructed, so carefully wrought, so economical that it is exceedingly difficult to penetrate. But, at the same time, it always rewards careful examination. Press at any point and it reveals the most subtle connections, the most insightful development of central ideas. Perhaps the most powerful and attractive feature of the *Tractatus* is that it represents the rigorous, unrelenting, and uncompromising development of a single vision. The crystalline structure of that vision gives it a purity and beauty that unquestionably rivals the great philosophical schemes of the past.

Although every feature of the early thought is structured by transcendence, the problems become particularly apparent and acute when one focuses on the relation between the logical and ethical views. Wittgenstein thought that there was an intimate relation between a "right view of things" and being a "good person." This was not merely a "philosophical" thesis with him. It expressed itself in his personal life and is clearly stated in one of his letters to Paul Engelmann. "I . . . wish I were a better man and had a better mind. These two things are really the same" (*LLW* p. 5). For Wittgenstein there is an essential connection between intellect and will or between seeing the world aright and willing it aright. This means that his account of language and the world becomes a key to an account of "right willing" or ethics. In fact, his account of language and the world provides the form for his ethical views. Just as the metaphysical subject apprehends the world as the totality of facts, so it is the task of the "ethical subject" to will the world as the totality of facts.

It is precisely when Wittgenstein's ethical views are spelled out in detail that one begins to suspect that there is a deep ambiguity embedded in the very notion of transcendence. In fact, it will be shown that Wittgenstein's ethical views require a notion of transcendence that is inconsistent with that required on the logical side. In the final analysis the *Tractatus* cannot be thought of as a coherent whole.

The failure of the *Tractatus* is not a failure of the writer. It is an inherent aspect of the vision itself, which is brought to light just because Wittgenstein so rigorously and brilliantly articulates the vision. What is striking (from our post-*Investigations* vantage point) is that the Wittgenstein of the *Tractatus* was fully aware of the internal tension but saw in it, not the failure of the project, but its final fulfillment, for he had managed to "put everything firmly in place by being silent about it." However, since much needs to be "said" in order to give meaning to and justify such a silence, there can be no fulfillment of the project.

The attempt to think and will from the transcendental point of view is finally and unavoidably incoherent. What it requires us to do is to treat ourselves both as individuals in the world and as transcendental subjects seeing and willing the world from outside as "the totality of facts." We are, at one and the same time, individuals— items in the world—and "conditions of possibility of the world." The ethical and logical goal of the *Tractatus* is to achieve a relation to the world such that "there are two godheads: the world and my independent I" (*NB* p. 74, 8.7.16). This requires on its logical side the apprehension of the world as a limited totality. Ethically it involves not merely that apprehension but the willful appropriation of the whole as an aesthetic object. Of course, the subject apprehending or appropriating must be set over against and beyond the "totality of facts," that is, the world. It must be a transcendental subject. At the same time, this "independent I"—this godhead—as actually achieved, is a particular thinking and willing individual situated within that totality. The project of the *Tractatus* as a theory of language, as an account of the world, and as an ethical vision is "the project to become God." But that project is incoherent. The *Tractatus* cannot be written because the perspective from which it would have to be written is said to be inaccessible on the basis of "seeing" what can only be seen from that perspective.

The later philosophy takes its inspiration from the failure of the *Tractatus*. The perspective of the *Philosophical Investigations* is not "the limit of the world." Its subject is not a "transcendental subject." It is a situated community of individual language users in the midst of things, sharing a common "form of life." The "problems and methods of philosophy" are recast in light of that, including the problem of the relation between language and the world. Specifically, a philosophical voice must be developed that speaks in a way that is consistent with its own limits. In the final sections of this volume I will sketch out the implications of this change of perspective, but a full development must wait upon another volume.

The next three chapters are an exposition of the logical aspects of the *Tractatus*. Scholars who are familiar with the *Tractatus* will not find a great deal of original interpretation in them. I merely set out those aspects of the logical doctrines that are essential for a full understanding of Wittgenstein's ethical thinking. My discussions of "elucidations" and the "metaphysical subject" are the most important and the most distinctive parts because the notion of transcendence can be brought into clearest focus there. Beginning with Chapter 5, I turn my attention to a careful explication of the ethical dimensions of Wittgenstein's early thought. This is relatively uncharted territory, and those chapters, therefore, represent a substantially new contribution to the understanding of Wittgenstein's philosophy.

2

THE THEORY OF LANGUAGE

AND LOGIC

What is the Tractarian question concerning language? There are various ways to formulate it. For example, it can be expressed as the question: What is the difference between sense and nonsense? This formulation is suggested by Wittgenstein's own characterization of the *Tractatus* cited in Chapter 1. Notice that this question presupposes that there is such a difference and that some marks or sounds have a sense or are meaningful. This leads to another way of formulating the question: What must be in order for there to be a meaningful language? This formulation has the advantage of focusing our attention on the relation between meaning and what is. Notice that it also presupposes that there is a meaningful language.

For Wittgenstein in the *Tractatus*, there is no skepticism about meaning. Language is meaningful or, what comes to the same thing in the *Tractatus*, language represents the world. To claim that language represents the world is not to make any claim about a theory of truth (although one is surely implied by Wittgenstein's account). Rather, the question of truth rests on the presupposition that certain marks and sounds under consideration already say something. For a sentence to be true or false, it must make a claim or say something about the world. And it is just this possibility of "saying something" that is the focus of attention in the *Tractatus*. What must language and the world be like in order for it to be possible to say something?

The second formulation above will suffice to guide us into the theory of language and logic in the *Tractatus*. Wittgenstein sketches an account of the world as the "totality of facts." He then explains language as a means of picturing facts to ourselves (*T* 2.1). Of course, neither is independent. Each is developed as a mirror image of the other. What this means will become clearer as we examine Wittgenstein's theory of language.

Language in the *Tractatus*

The most basic units of meaning in the *Tractatus* are referred to as "atomic propositions." The units are "atomic" because, as a matter of definition, each is logically independent of every other proposition. If the truth of a given proposition follows from, or depends upon, the truth of another, it is not atomic. Atomic propositions are simple in the sense that they do not have any other propositions as elements. Atomic propositions are complex in the sense that they are concatenations of names that stand for simple objects (*T* 4.22). However, "only propositions have sense; only in the nexus of a proposition does a name have meaning" (*T* 3.3). Corresponding to an atomic sentence is an atomic fact, state of affairs, or situation, which is itself a concatenation of simple objects. Each such state of affairs is independent of every other (*T* 2.061). Just as names have meaning only in the context of atomic propositions, simple objects are essentially the possibilities of states of affairs (*T* 2.011).

Thus Wittgenstein proposes an ontology of facts (*T* 1.1) as well as a theory of meaning that takes the proposition as the basic unit. There is a straightforward parallelism of structure. Names correspond to simple objects, propositions correspond to facts; propositions are structured sets of names, facts are structured sets of objects;

and, finally, names have meaning only in the context of propositions, and objects just are the possibilities of facts.

The relation between an atomic sentence and the corresponding fact is that of picturing: "We picture facts to ourselves" (*T* 2.1). We can do this because both propositions and facts are structured arrangements of elements. In this sense, propositions are also facts. But there is an important difference between a fact that is a proposition and a fact that is *in the world*. The structure of a fact that is a proposition is a function of conventions that determine which aspects of a set of marks are symbols and which aspects represent relations. This is why the structure of the facts represented cannot be read off the mere spatial arrangement of marks (except in special cases). Without the conventions governing a particular language, there is nothing to determine what its arrangement represents. The relation between a particular language and the world is in no sense a natural relation. Of course, Wittgenstein is not interested in the particulars of such conventions. They are of interest to psychology or linguistics or philology but not to the project of the *Tractatus*. For that inquiry he is interested only in those aspects that are necessary to any system of representation whatsoever, no matter which particular conventions give it specific form.

This is important because it forces us to see that picturing as it is used in the *Tractatus* is not a natural relation. There may be cases in which we think we are reading a pictured fact from a linguistic picture without referring to conventions. However, such readings are at best limiting cases and do not offer a comprehensive understanding of the notion of a "logical" picture. In such cases it can be shown that we are generalizing from features that are not essential to representation or picturing as such.

The notion at the heart of the concept of a picture is that some elements in the picture represent or stand in for elements in the fact depicted. Wittgenstein says, "The possibility of propositions [pictures] is based on the principle that objects have signs as their representatives" (*T* 4.0312). Two aspects of the Tractarian doctrine of objects help clarify that claim. Objects are or have both form and content.

The Form of Objects

Wittgenstein says, "The possibility of its occurring in states of affairs is the form of an object" (*T* 2.0141). Simple signs name simple objects, but naming in the *Tractatus* is not merely a matter of attaching a label to something that is itself "atomic" and so independent of other objects. As has already been pointed out, "it is essential to things (objects) that they should be possible constituents in states of affairs" (*T* 2.011). In other words, objects cannot be conceived independently of the complexes (facts) into which they may enter. An object is the possibility of certain combinations. So when the object is given, all its possible combinations are also given (*T* 2.0123). There is a sense then, in which we cannot distinguish two things—objects and the possible combinations into which they may enter. (Why this is not true *simpliciter* will be made clear in the discussion of "content.") Similarly, names (the proxies of objects) cannot appear in two different roles "by themselves and in propositions" (*T* 2.0122). What it means for a given sign to name an object is that the sign can meaningfully enter into a particular range of atomic propositions. This is why Wittgenstein's conception of the name of a simple object already involves the sine qua non of picturing—structure or form. Consider an ordinary picture, say, a painting of a ship in the harbor. It is obviously not enough for such a picture to contain a number of elements equal to what it pictures. In fact, it is not even clear what could be meant by "elements" if at least minimal structural considerations are not brought into play. What will be isomorphic with what? What are to count as elements? A dab of red paint taken in relation to other elements of this painting may be a sun. That same dab in another painting may be something else or even nothing at all—a smudge, for example, mistakenly made by the painter. Even in an ordinary painting, therefore, we cannot isolate naming (the fact that the red dab stands for the sun) from formal considerations (the relations in which that dab stands to other elements of the painting). We might paraphrase Wittgenstein here by saying that a painting of the sun cannot occur in two separate roles: by itself and in a painting.

A mere collection of colored dots is not by itself a picture. The structural relations among the elements constitute the determinate nature of the picture. As Wittgenstein says, "What constitutes a picture is that its elements are related to one another in a determinate way" (T 2.14). Since, in a given fact, simple objects necessarily stand in a determinate relation to each other, that relation must also be present among the names in the atomic sentence. It is precisely in virtue of the common form of possible fact and sentence that there can be logical pictures, that is, meaning. A logical picture or proposition is an instance of the same structure or form that is present in the fact it represents (T 2.203). Wittgenstein says, "A propositional sign is a fact. A proposition is not a medley of words.—(Just as a theme in music is not a medley of notes.) A proposition is articulated. Only facts can express a sense, a set of names cannot" (T 3.142). Of course, strictly taken, there cannot be a mere "set of names," at least not where the names of simple objects are concerned, because as we have just pointed out, names cannot appear in two different roles—by themselves and in propositions.

Two points must be clarified here. First, when Wittgenstein says that a picture is a fact (T 3.142, also see 2.14 and 2.16), he introduces a serious ambiguity. On the one hand, the fact in question might be thought to be an arrangement of elements taken as mere physical objects. But that would be deeply misleading. There would be no nonarbitrary way to identify the so-called elements of the picture. Why pick the physically distinct items as elements? Wouldn't that be arbitrary? If we are dealing only with physical objects, why not consider their top and bottom halves as elements? Further, how would we distinguish items "accidentally present," perhaps a water drop, from meaningful elements? Clearly, at this level there would be no nonarbitrary way to identify the "elements" of the picture as a fact.

What is required is that the elements of the picture be identified by reference to their role in the picture *taken as a picture*. To know what are the "elements" of a picture is already to know which groups of physical components are significant. And this implies that a picture is not a mere collection of physical objects—"picture" and "physical object" operate on different logical levels. (The bearing of this point on Wittgenstein's overall view will be discussed in detail in Chapter 4, "The Metaphysical Subject.") And this means that the kind of fact that a picture is in virtue of being a picture is different from the kind of fact that a picture is in virtue of being an arrangement of physical objects. This is true even though the picture is, after all, an arrangement of physical objects.

Second, this understanding of the claim that a picture is a fact clarifies the contention at 2.203 that a picture *contains* the possibility of the situation it represents. If the elements of a picture are determined by what parts of the sentence are meaningful, that is to say, names, we see that the question of "logical form" is not a question about what physical combinations are physically possible. That Wittgenstein understands the matter this way is quite clear from what he says at 2.1513: "So a picture, conceived in this way [as a model of reality], also includes the pictorial relationship, which makes it into a picture." And what is this "pictorial relationship"? Wittgenstein tells us in the very next statement. "The pictorial relationship consists of the correlations of the picture's elements with things" (*T* 2.1514). So when Wittgenstein says that "a picture is a fact," he means it is a fact when taken as a picture and that it already includes "the pictorial relationship" that is "the correlations of the picture's elements with things." Those correlations set the possibilities: "If I know an object I also know all its possible occurrences in states of affairs. (Every one of these possibilities must be part of the nature of the object.) A new possibility cannot be discovered later" (*T* 2.0122). Logical form is a matter of what arrangements of meaningful units are logically possible. This already presupposes that those "meaning units" stand for the objects they do. Questions of logical form are not independent of naming. For a name to stand for such and such an object just is for it to be able to enter meaningfully into certain combinations and not others.

So when Wittgenstein says that a picture contains the possibility of the situation it represents, he means the picture taken as a picture. As a picture it contains meaningful elements that are logically arranged in exactly the manner that the objects its elements represent would be arranged if it were true. So it contains the possibility of that situation. It does so because as a picture it is an instance of that arrangement, although it differs in content from the state of affairs it represents. This is exactly what Wittgenstein means by saying that sentence and corresponding fact share logical form.

Let us now return to the main thread of our discussion. Wittgenstein contends that the possibility of pictures, and therefore of language, depends on the fact that objects have linguistic representatives in names. This means that simple objects in their possible combinations constitute the unalterable precondition of meaning.

> Objects make up the substance of the world. That is why they cannot be composite.
>
> If the world had no substance, then whether a proposition had sense would depend on whether another proposition was true.
>
> In that case we could not sketch out any picture of the world (true or false). (*T* 2.021–2.0212)

For the Wittgenstein of the *Tractatus*, meaning must be determined by that which is prior to all questions of fact, since a question of fact can arise only if meaningful language is already in place. It follows immediately that it cannot be a matter of fact that objects exist. Since objects are a necessary precondition for the possibility of meaning, it can make no sense either to assert or deny that they exist.

This should explain why Wittgenstein holds that states of affairs cannot be named and objects can only be named. (See T 3.144 and 3.221.) As we have just seen, an object is presupposed by the meaningfulness of its name so that a name is essentially "univalent." "Names are like points" (T 3.144). If there is no object, the "name" in question is meaningless. So, of course, the pseudo-proposition "X does not exist," where X purports to name an object, is meaningless, as is its contradictory. If "X does not exist" were significant, it would require X to name an object, which it cannot do as a condition of its truth. Simply put, if it is true, it is meaningless since there is nothing for X to name. If, on the other hand, it is meaningful, it is false since X is meaningful, and so the object named by it must exist. And, of course, the pseudo-proposition "X exists" would be true if meaningful, and meaningless if false. But that is absurd.

Although names are "univalent," it is essential to propositions that they can be either *true or false,* that is to say, bivalent. This is what Wittgenstein means when he says that if names are like points, "propositions [are] like arrows" (T 3.144). There is, following the determination that something is an arrow, the further question of which way it points. This essential bivalence is the direct result of the picture theory itself. "A picture agrees with reality or fails to agree; it is correct or incorrect, true or false" (T 2.21). So for any proposition or picture, "what . . . [it] . . . represents it represents independently of its truth or falsity, by means of its pictorial form" (T 2.22). Since the meaningfulness of a proposition is presupposed by its being either true or false, the conditions for that meaningfulness must be independent of its truth or its falsity. If a proposition were treated as the description of an object rather than of a fact, the falsity of the proposition would mean that the object does not exist—a case in which the condition for the falsity of the description would also be the condition for its meaninglessness. Similarly, if the linguistic expression of a state of affairs were treated as a name, it would be impossible to "refer" to the state of affairs without presupposing its existence. That in turn would require a "necessarily existent state of affairs," which is absurd.

To avoid such results Wittgenstein maintains a sharp distinction between naming and describing. "Objects can only be *named*. Signs are their representatives. I can only speak *about* them: I cannot *put them into words*. Propositions can only say *how* things are, not *what* they are" (*T* 3.221). A state of affairs can be put into words, at least in one sense. An atomic fact is a structured set of objects, and the corresponding proposition is a structured set of names. As we have seen earlier and as Wittgenstein says at 2.161, "there must be something identical in a picture and what it depicts, to enable the one to be a picture of the other at all." The structure present in the state of affairs must be present in the proposition as well. So the state of affairs is actually "put into words." Objects cannot reappear in the proposition; they can only have proxies. They cannot be put into words.

The priority of objects over all states of affairs follows directly from the very nature of the problem with which the *Tractatus* begins: the problem of articulating the relation between the world and language understood as the possibility of representation. Any account of meaning that presupposes the truth (and therefore meaningfulness) of some proposition would, ipso facto, fail as a response to that problem. It would not be comprehensive enough because it must be an account of the meaningfulness of all propositions, whereas the class of meaningful propositions is obviously larger than the class of true propositions. The priority of objects over any actual state of affairs insures the independence and priority of meaning over truth. (See *T* 2.014, 2.024, 2.027.) Since the realm of the possible is fixed once and for all in virtue of the objects that constitute it, meaningful but false atomic propositions are possible. A false proposition pictures a possible combination of objects that, as things happen, does not obtain, but it (the proposition) is, nonetheless, meaningful in virtue of its containing names of objects arranged in a configuration that mirrors a possible combination of the objects the names represent.

The Content of Objects

Though this completes the discussion of the form of objects, it is not yet a comprehensive account either of objects or of their role in making picturing possible. As was pointed out, a name has reference only in the context of a proposition, and this means that for a to name the object O is for a to play a certain role in a proposition or range of propositions. Consider $\exists x\,(Px)$. Its truth conditions can be represented as the set of elementary propositions "$Pa \vee Pb \vee Pc\ldots$." Now setting aside difficulties with this sort of proposal, what is the difference between "Pa" and "Pb"? Certainly a and b play *the same role* in the two propositions unless, of course, by "different role" one means that a names O-1 while b names O-2. There is no other difference in role that can bring out the difference between the two atomic propositions since by hypothesis a can meaningfully complete any proposition that b can. In other words, the claim that when a names O-1 is equivalent to a playing a certain role in a proposition is true only in an utterly trivial sense.

To get a better understanding of the issues here, we need to take a close look at T 2.0141 and following.

> The possibility of its occurring in states of affairs is the form of an object.
> Objects make up the substance of the world. . . .
> The substance of the world can only determine a form, and not any material properties. . . .
> It [substance] is form and content. (T 2.0141, 2.021, 2.0231, 2.025)

These passages make it clear that objects are the substance of the world and that substance is both form and content. However, Wittgenstein also claims that substance "can only determine a form and not any material properties" of the world. It appears, therefore, that there are two sets of distinctions at work, one between form and material properties and the other between form and content. This somewhat problematic use of terms can be clarified as follows.

Both form and content are aspects of the substance of the world, in contrast to its material properties. By "material properties" Wittgenstein clearly means the actual facts (see T 2.0231). It is a material property that "Pa" obtains. That, of course, cannot be determined a priori and so cannot be determined by the substance of the world. That there are two distinct possible states of affairs "Pa" and "Pb" is a matter determined by the substance of the world independently of the world's material properties. But both the form and the content of all possible facts (the form of the world = objects) are prior to the world (the totality of actual facts = material properties).

The previous account of objects has not yet taken into consideration the claim that they are content as well as form. In fact, it is by no means easy to see what can be meant by "content" at this stage. Clearly, the requirement that there be atomic facts and objects is in no sense an empirical discovery. Wittgenstein did not first stumble onto objects and then discover them to be constituents of all facts. Something of that sort may be what some of the logical positivists hoped they saw in the *Tractatus*. For them, the analysis in terms of objects was colored by certain epistemological doctrines. However, Wittgenstein's procedure is rigorously a priori and deductive. For example, he says, "Even if the world is infinitely complex, so that every fact consists in infinitely many states of affairs and every state of affairs is composed of infinitely many objects, there would still have to be objects and states of affairs" (T 4.2211). Obviously, if the world were infinitely complex, no actual analysis would ever arrive at atomic facts or the simple objects that constitute them. Nonetheless, there must be both simple objects and their names if there is to be determinate sense. "The requirement that simple signs be possible is the requirement that sense be determinate" (T 3.23). Further, there is no such thing as indeterminate sense. This is not to deny that there are ambiguous or vague sentences. Of course there are. However, such sentences do not have *a* sense. For an atomic proposition to have *a* sense is for it to picture *a* fact. So there must be one and only one fact pictured by every atomic proposition.

Just as objects are not discoveries of some process of investigation but rather are deductive products of the fundamental Tractarian scheme, so also the view that the substance of the world is both form and content follows directly from aspects of language understood within that scheme. It is not a discovery made through an examination of representative objects but a deduction drawn from the nature of distinct atomic propositions. We can see this in the argument that sets the problem for us.

If "Pa" is an atomic proposition and a is a name and if "Pb" is an atomic proposition and b is a name, then either "Pa" and "Pb" have the same meaning or they do not. But if they mean the same, then a and b mean the same, and in an ideal language they would not both be included. Certainly in that case "Pa" and "Pb" would not be two distinct propositions in the expansion of "$\exists x$ (Px)." On the other hand, if they have different meanings, then a and b must name different objects since "a name means an object. The object is its meaning" (T 3.203). If there is a difference in meaning at this level, there are different objects. However, the difference cannot be one of form since O-1 and O-2 are both possible constituents in the same range of facts and therefore have the same form. Thus there must be another sort of difference—a difference in "content" determined by objects.

There are a number of other passages throughout the *Tractatus* in which the distinction between form and content plays a central role. (See, for example, T 5.5302 and T 5.526.) However, *Tractatus* 3.13 deserves special attention. Wittgenstein says, "a proposition contains the form, but not the content of its sense." A propositional sign is itself a fact (T 3.14), and as such it contains the form of the fact that it pictures. However, the constituents of the representing fact (the proposition) and the represented fact (the state of affairs) are not and cannot be the same. Again, we have sameness in form and difference in content. In fact, it is the very possibility of this difference that makes picturing possible since to be a picture is to be specifically different from what is pictured (T 2.173).

We can now see that it is only in virtue of being *both form and content* that objects named make picturing possible. A picture cannot be a picture for Wittgenstein unless it has its form in common with what it pictures. "What any picture, of whatever form, must have in common with reality, in order to be able to depict it—correctly or incorrectly—in any way at all, is logical form, i.e. the form of reality" (T 2.18). If proposition and fact do not share a common form, the one cannot picture the other. If, on the other hand, they share form *and* content, there will be no difference between fact and proposition. In such a case we would have a map that is identical with what it maps, which is no map at all.

But now what is the difference between the objects O-1 and O-2? This difference is, in principle, unstatable. Suppose that we try to state the difference between the two by saying that O-1 is a constituent of the fact expressed by "*Pa*" while O-2 is a constituent of the fact expressed by "*Pb*." This clearly will not do because we cannot specify the difference between "*Pa*" and "*Pb*" except in virtue of the difference in meaning between *a* and *b,* and this can be explicated only in terms of the difference in the objects O-1 and O-2 since, again, "A name means an object. The object is its meaning." There is no independent access to either aspect here. Differences between objects are explicated by reference to the differences between propositions that include their names. At the same time, differences between propositions are explicated by reference to the objects named in them. Thus, objects require propositions for their explication and

propositions require objects for their explication. The difference between the two objects O-1 and O-2 can be "shown" only by the
fact that *a* has a different meaning from *b*. It is not accessible in
any other way. Wittgenstein is perfectly clear on the point: "Thus
one proposition 'fa' *shows* that the object a occurs in its sense, two
propositions 'fa' and 'ga' show that the same object is mentioned in
both of them" (*T* 4.1211, my emphasis). And by the same reason-
ing we can say that "P*a*" and "P*b*" show that different objects are
mentioned in each of them. However,

> If two objects have the same logical form, the only distinction
> between them, apart from their external properties, is that they
> are different.
> Either a thing has properties that nothing else has, in which
> case we can immediately use a description to distinguish it from
> the others and refer to it; or, on the other hand, there are several
> things that have the whole set of their properties in common,
> in which case it is quite impossible to indicate one of them.
> For if there is nothing to distinguish a thing, I cannot distin-
> guish it, since if I do it will be distinguished after all. (*T* 2.0233–
> 2.02331)

It follows that for objects, at least, Wittgenstein is committed to
denying the principle of the identity of indiscernibles (not, of course,
the principle of the indiscernibility of identicals). That is, O-1 and
O-2 just are different, and that is shown by the difference in the
meaning of "P*a*" and "P*b*." However, there is no way to specify that
difference which does not already presuppose it. So it follows on this
point at least that "What *can* be shown, *cannot* be said" (*T* 4.1212).
Here we encounter for the first time Wittgenstein's famous distinction between showing and saying. The distinction between form
and content depends on that distinction, on a difference that can
be shown but cannot be said. This is an important result because

the very possibility of picturing depends on the distinction between form and content as applied to objects. And, of course, the picture theory is Wittgenstein's solution to the problem that is the defining task of the *Tractatus*—the problem of the relation between language and the world. Whatever is implicated in the distinction between form and content is absolutely pivotal for an understanding of the *Tractatus*.

The showing/saying distinction appears at critical points throughout the *Tractatus*. That the coherence of the entire work depends upon it will be demonstrated in the course of this study. What we have seen so far is that the distinction is crucial for the *Tractatus*' theory of meaning. Without the showing/saying distinction we have no access to the form/content distinction and, without that, representation or picturing cannot even be explicated. This is not to say that the showing/saying distinction solves the problems of form and content. However, it is to say that the fate of the one distinction is tied to that of the other.

Propositions and Logic in the *Tractatus*

At 4.5 Wittgenstein says, "The general form of a proposition is: This is how things stand." Every proposition expresses a possible fact—a state of affairs. It is true if things stand in the way it claims they stand and it is false if they do not. While the meaning of any proposition is a function of the state of affairs that would obtain if it were true, it must be possible to determine what it means without determining whether what is being claimed is true (*T* 4.024). Two further "facts" follow from this. First, "A proposition must restrict reality to two alternatives: yes or no" (*T* 4.023), but since "there are no pictures that are true *a priori*" (*T* 2.225), no propositions can restrict reality to anything less than two alternatives. This follows immediately from the "fact" that an atomic proposition is a picture and that every picture "represents its subject from a position outside it" (*T* 2.173). So for any genuine picture, its being a picture is independent of its being a representation of an actual state of affairs. Simply put, things can fail to be the way they are pictured. This means that every genuine proposition must be true or false and no genuine proposition can be necessarily true or necessarily false.

Wittgenstein's treatment of "necessary truth" follows from these insights. Since no genuine proposition can be necessarily true or false, it follows immediately that any "proposition" that is necessarily true or false is not genuine. It does not picture a fact. At this point, it is important to introduce the difference between elementary, or atomic, propositions and complex propositions. Each elementary proposition is not only logically independent of every other elementary proposition, it is also simple in the sense that it contains no other propositions as components. Of course, these two features are not independent of each other. It is partly because atomic propositions are simple that they are taken to be independent. Or, at least, the contrapositive is true. If they were not simple, they would not be logically independent. For example, "Hodges knows that *P*" cannot be an atomic proposition simply because its truth is not independent of the truth of *P*.

It is important to point out that the logical independence of elementary propositions is not an empirical discovery. There are certainly real problems about the status of any given proposition as atomic, and Wittgenstein offers no examples of such propositions. In any case, however, one cannot refute Wittgenstein's contention here by producing a counterexample, namely, a proposition that is atomic but whose truth is dependent on the truth of another proposition. If the truth of one depends on the truth of another, it is not atomic. This again confirms the a priori character of the fundamental claims of the *Tractatus*.

Every elementary proposition is a picture of a possible state of affairs, and "if an elementary proposition is true, the state of affairs exists: if an elementary proposition is false, the state of affairs does not exist" (*T* 4.25). There are no necessarily true elementary propositions. Complex propositions are built up out of elementary ones by way of truth-functional operations so that the truth of any complex is always a function of the truth of its component elementary propositions. But,

> Among the possible groups of truth-conditions there are two extreme cases.
> In one of these cases the proposition is true for all the truth-possibilities of the elementary propositions. We say that the truth-conditions are tautological.
> In the second case the proposition is false for all the truth-possibilities: the truth-conditions are contradictory. (*T* 4.46)

All necessary propositions are either tautologies or contradictions. Moreover, "tautologies and contradictions are not pictures of reality. They do not represent any possible situations" (*T* 4.462). Therefore necessary truths are not genuine "propositions" at all. "Tautology and contradiction are the limiting cases—indeed the disintegration —of the combination of signs" (*T* 4.466).

It does not follow that tautologies or contradictions are strictly nonsensical. After all, the claim that they have no sense must be understood in terms of the theory of meaning developed in the *Tractatus*. All Wittgenstein is at pains to show is that they do not "picture states of affairs." "Tautologies and contradictions are not, however, nonsensical. They are part of the symbolism, just as 'o' is part of the symbolism of arithmetic" (*T* 4.4611). What Wittgenstein seems to mean here by "part of the symbolism" is that tautologies contain essentially only logical constants such that any elementary propositions (or, for that matter, any propositions) may fill the gaps without affecting the resultant truth values. In this way tautologies "show" the logic of the relations among all possible descriptions without being themselves descriptions. Now, if all tautologies and contradictions contain only logical constants, it follows immediately that they cannot be genuine propositions, for Wittgenstein says,

> The possibility of propositions is based on the principle that objects have signs as their representatives.
>
> My fundamental idea is that the 'logical constants' are not representatives; that there can be no representatives of the *logic* of facts. (*T* 4.0312)

There are no "logical objects"; logical constants are not names; since tautologies essentially contain only logical constants, they cannot be propositions—they do not picture any structured combination of objects.

This provides us with the key to Wittgenstein's claim at *T* 6.13:

> Logic is not a body of doctrine, but a mirror-image of the world.
>
> Logic is transcendental.

What Wittgenstein means by "transcendental" here is that the "propositions" of logic express the limits of all possible saying. However, they express those limits not by stating what the limits are, which cannot be done, but by being *without content*. This "shows" that "at this point" nothing can be said. That there are and must be tautologies "shows" what the limits of language are. It shows this by showing when it is impossible to say anything.

The existence of tautologies and contradictions is a necessary aspect of any symbolism that depends on the fact that "although there is something arbitrary in our notation, *this* much is not arbitrary—that *when* we have determined one thing arbitrarily, something else is necessarily the case. (This derives from the *essence* of notation.)" (*T* 3.342). But if tautologies are connected to the "essence of notation," then by being essentially *without content,* that is, essentially failing to picture anything, they show the limits of all possible representation. They do this by showing that there can be no logical fact since the description of such a "fact" is without "subject matter" (*T* 6.124). If the tautologies show the limits of all "subject matter," that is, the limits of all possible facts, then they show the limits of the world. This is what Wittgenstein means when he says that logic is a "mirror-image of the world" (*T* 6.13). It is a mirror image of the logical or formal features (*T* 6.12) of the world—what he also calls the "scaffolding of the world" (*T* 6.124).

Every proposition of logic must leave the whole range of possible facts completely open. And yet, "it is clear that something about the world must be indicated by the fact that certain combinations of symbols . . . are tautologies" (*T* 6.124). What is indicated can have nothing to do with which facts obtain. It indicates that there are facts or, to put the point in linguistic terms, "that names have meaning and elementary propositions sense" (*T* 6.124). Of course, when Wittgenstein says that "elementary propositions have sense," he is not making a claim about any particular language. He is merely speaking of the possibility of representation itself. But, in that case, his claim amounts to the claim that there is a world—a totality of fact—to be represented. So what the tautologies indicate about the world is that there is a world and that is not a further fact about the world. Actually, that is said to be something "mystical." (See *T* 6.44.) Again we have achieved a view of the world as "a limited whole" and in so doing discovered further evidence of the dependence of the logical aspects of the *Tractatus* on its "mystical vision." More will be said about this in a moment.

Remember that each atomic fact is logically independent of every other atomic fact. No inference can be made from one atomic fact to any other. This may seem obviously false in the case of P and ∼P. Can't we infer from the truth of P to the falsity of ∼P, and vice versa? Here, however, we confront Wittgenstein's "fundamental idea" that the " 'logical constants' are not representatives" (*T* 4.0312). There is no object named by "not" to be a possible constituent of atomic facts. Only one atomic fact makes P true and ~P false. There cannot be a distinct fact corresponding to ~P since there is no object corresponding to "not." The pictured content of each is the same. In the one case it is affirmed and in the other it is denied. But now to generalize, if the logical constants are not representatives, there can be no "logical facts," that is to say, facts that contain only logical objects. Propositions that contain only logical constants cannot "say," that is, picture anything.

So logic is transcendental in the sense that it expresses the limits of language. It does not say what those limits are; it does not even say that there are limits. However, logic does give linguistic expression to the limits through the existence of tautologies. But why does Wittgenstein suppose that tautologies reveal something about the essence of language? How do we get from an interesting feature of certain specific formal languages to a contention about the "limits of all possible representation?" The answer is that the philosophical importance of tautologies is already seen in terms of a "transcendental project." We saw a moment ago that Wittgenstein's doctrine of tautologies presupposes that the world can be seen as "a limited whole." The claim that the tautologies express the limits of all possible representation already presupposes the notion of transcendence at the heart of the Tractarian project. The tautologies can be taken to express the limits of all possible representation only if we suppose that it is possible to take "language as a whole," if it is possible to construe what is a feature of "this language" as "essential to all notations." Language must be taken as an *object given complete* possessing limits that can be shown in some way. The point is one about the philosophical significance of tautologies. They can be given "transcendental significance" only if the "transcendental point of view" is already presupposed. Otherwise, the existence of tautologies will merely be an interesting feature of certain "formal languages." But it will not "show" the essential features of any possible language. So "logic is transcendental" if and only if it is seen in terms of a project that presupposes transcendence. It is only from that point of view that the tautologies "show" the "limits of all possible language." Wherever we find the showing/saying distinction at work, we also find transcendence presupposed. What is shown is what would be "seen" by a transcendental subject—in this case, a subject for which language appears as a "limited whole."

We now have a complete account of the nature of propositions. All elementary propositions are pictures of actual or possible states of affairs. Such picturing is made possible because elements of reality (objects) have proxies that stand in the proposition in the logical order found among the objects in the world. All nonelementary propositions are built up from elementary ones via truth-functional connectives and so have their truth determined by the values assigned to the elementary ones. Finally, apparent necessary truths are mere "disintegrations" of the system of connectives. This is why Wittgenstein can say that the general form of a proposition is: this is how things stand.

One natural objection to this account of propositions is that it simply has nothing to do with ordinary everyday language. Even though there is nothing like a crystalline structure in the mass of ordinary language, we do grasp its meaning. The *Tractatus*, therefore, cannot be an account of meaning in everyday language but of an "ideal" language, as Russell suggests in his introduction (*T* p. ix). But, as if in anticipation of this contention, Wittgenstein writes, "All the propositions of our everyday language are actually in perfect logical order just as they are" (*T* 5.5563). The theory of meaning and language presented in the *Tractatus* is the theory of the meaning of language as such, not of some particular language—ideal or otherwise. If an everyday proposition is a proposition, then it "says something," and if it "says something," it must have its logical form in common with the state of affairs that it represents. This is true of it just as it stands!

Every ordinary proposition is analyzable into atomic propositions or truth-functional complexes of such propositions. The only alternative to this would be to suggest that each and every ordinary "proposition" was not a genuine proposition. But surely this is ruled out! To have a meaning just is to be either an atomic proposition that directly pictures a state of affairs or to be a truth function of atomic propositions. This is true for *all* propositions, including everyday ones. So if an everyday proposition is a proposition, it is in order just as it is.

Of course, it does not follow that we can determine what atomic sentence is involved by simply inspecting the everyday proposition. Grammatical form is not a good guide to logical form.

Everyday language is a part of the human organism and is no less complicated than it.

It is not humanly possible to gather immediately from it what the logic of language is.

Language disguises thought. So much so, that from the outward form of the clothing it is impossible to infer the form of the thought beneath it, because the outward form of the clothing is not designed to reveal the form of the body, but for entirely different purposes. (*T* 4.002)

It is this failure of grammatical form to reveal logical form that gives rise to "fundamental confusions" of which "the whole of philosophy is full" (*T* 3.324). It is also this failure that allows Wittgenstein to see the task of philosophy as one of clarifying the propositions of ordinary discourse, including those of science. A "logical syntax" would allow us to avoid errors by making the "clothing" reveal the actual form it covers. In a language governed by logical grammar, logical and grammatical form would coincide; it is clear that ordinary language is not perfect in that sense. But it does not follow from this that everyday propositions are not in perfect logical order.

Given Wittgenstein's account of the meaning of both significant propositions—elementary propositions and truth functions of them —and tautologies, an important question remains unresolved. How are the propositions of the *Tractatus* to be understood? Can they be fitted into the analysis Wittgenstein has presented? That is the topic of the next chapter.

3

PHILOSOPHY, ELUCIDATIONS,

AND SHOWING/SAYING

The Status of the Propositions of the *Tractatus*

Given the previous account of the nature of propositions, what can we say of the "propositions" that are the account itself? What of the claims that objects constitute the unalterable form of reality and that the general form of a proposition is: This is how things stand. Can these be propositions? They seem to tell us something about the way things must stand if language is to be possible. But insofar as they express necessary conditions for the possibility of meaning and in doing so are meaningful, their very meaningfulness requires their truth. That is, they appear to be examples of "pictures that are true a priori."

The problem may be put like this. Whatever can be said could be otherwise. This is simply a version of the claims discussed earlier that (1) every genuine proposition must be either true or false, and (2) no genuine proposition can be necessarily true or necessarily false. Therefore, if what makes saying possible can itself be said, then it also could be otherwise. But if it were otherwise, there could be no saying that it was. So either one cannot say what makes saying possible or it is false that whatever can be said can be otherwise.

And that would mean that the "propositions" of the *Tractatus* cannot both say something and be true. The "language" of the *Tractatus* is a language that transcends the limits of language. It is a language that is not a language on its own terms.

Wittgenstein's suggestion, in the preface to the *Tractatus*, that one can set the limits of language but not the limits of thought does not seem correct. If it would require thinking the unthinkable in order to set the limits to thought, then it must require saying the unsayable in order to set the limits of language. So, either "what lies on the other side of the limit" is *not* simply nonsense (in which case "the limit" is not the limit), or the *Tractatus* is simply nonsense.

At 4.114 Wittgenstein proposes a method for setting the limits to what can be thought that may be designed to avoid the above argument. He says,

> It [Philosophy] must set limits to what can be thought; and, in doing so, to what cannot be thought.
> It must set limits to what cannot be thought by working outward through what can be thought.
> It will signify what cannot be said, by presenting clearly what can be said. (*T* 4.114–115)

This seems to be saying that since the limits of thought cannot be set by thinking both sides of the limit, they must be set from within "by working outward through what can be thought." But what does that suggestion really come to? There are only two possibilities. First, by "presenting clearly what can be said," Wittgenstein may mean simply making a list of meaningful propositions. (This could be the force of the methodological proposal at *T* 6.53, which is discussed below.) But any such list could not "set the limits to thought," for two independent reasons. On the one hand, for any actual list there would be disagreement about membership. Should the list include, for example, "The general form of a proposition is: This is how things stand"? For any *mere* list there can be no method to decide that question. And that means that such a list could set no interesting limit. On the other hand, any list would be essentially open ended. New members could always be added unless the list included the claim that its actual members were all the possible members. However, that claim could not be merely another member of the list. As a member it would have to be meaningful. But if it were, it would be either true or false and, since by hypothesis it sets the limits of membership for the list, it must be true. But then "whether a proposition had sense would depend on whether another proposition was true. In that case we could not sketch out any picture of the world (true or false)" (*T* 2.0211–212). This alternative leads nowhere.

Perhaps by "presenting clearly what can be said" Wittgenstein means giving some account of why the list has the members and only the members it does. However, that would force us to inquire about the status of such an account and thus leads back to the original argument. It follows that what Wittgenstein proposes in 4.114–115 cannot be interpreted in a way that will allow one both to set the limits of language and to escape the argument at hand.

That argument can now be stated in a more formal mode. Every genuine proposition has a contradictory that is a genuine proposition. Suppose that "P" asserts what it is that makes saying possible. That is, "P" is the *correct* answer to the question "What are the conditions for meaningfulness?" If "P" correctly asserts that C is the condition, then in order for "P" to be *meaningful*, C must obtain and be the condition of meaningfulness. Now consider the proposition "not Q," which asserts that condition C does not obtain. If that proposition is meaningful, then it must be false since C is the condition for meaningfulness. If "not Q" is true, then "not Q" is meaningless. This means that the meaningfulness of "not Q" entails the truth of "Q." Given that no genuine proposition can be necessarily false, it follows immediately that "not Q" is not a genuine proposition, and from this and the original hypothesis, it follows that "Q" is not a genuine proposition either. But "Q" by hypothesis is supposed to state that C, which is the condition for the possibility of meaningfulness, obtains. Of course, if "Q" is not a genuine proposition, "P" cannot be one. It follows from this that no genuine proposition can be a correct answer to the question "What are the conditions of meaningfulness?" But, "when the answer cannot be put into words, neither can the question be put into words" (*T* 6.5). So what "P" purports to say must not be sayable, and the question that is answered by "P" must be unaskable.

It is usual at this point to appeal to Wittgenstein's famous distinction between showing and saying. He certainly recognizes throughout the *Tractatus* that there is a great deal one cannot say but which nonetheless one can and must become aware of through the use of language. It is this that is shown. He says, "Propositions can represent the whole of reality, but they cannot represent what they must have in common with reality in order to be able to represent it—logical form" (*T* 4.12). Logical form cannot be *re-presented* by propositions because a proposition "represents its subject from a position outside of it" (*T* 2.173). What makes picturing possible is the essential difference between picture and what is pictured. "That is why a picture represents its subject correctly or incorrectly" (*T* 2.173). But logical form is that which all propositions have in virtue of being propositions, so "in order to be able to represent logical form, we should have to be able to station ourselves with propositions somewhere outside logic, that is to say outside the world" (*T* 4.12). Logical form, though not representable, is not beyond language. In fact, as we have seen, it is present in language.

> Propositions *show* the logical form of reality.
> They display it.
> Thus one proposition 'fa' shows that the object a occurs in its sense, two propositions 'fa' and 'ga' show that the same object is mentioned in both of them. (*T* 4.121–4.1211)

What is attractive about showing is that it is not bivalent in the way that saying must be since what is shown underlies both true and false saying. With regard to what language shows, there is *literally* no alternative. So, of course, no specific saying—nothing *in particular* that can be said—is to the philosophical point. "Philosophy does not result in 'philosophical propositions', but rather in the clarification of propositions" (*T* 4.112). What needs to be grasped is precisely what underlies every saying.

It is in light of this univalent character of showing that Wittgenstein believed that he really had solved the problems of philosophy once and for all! It explains why he thought the value of the *Tractatus* was simply a matter of whether "the nail has been hit on the head" (*T* preface, p. 4). As he puts it, the truth of his insights is "unassailable and definitive" (*T* preface, p. 5) since it is just a matter of seeing what is there to be seen. There can be no alternative or argument. But, of course, he may not have successfully conveyed that seeing to his readers simply because his "powers are too slight for the accomplishment" (*T* preface, p. 5).

It is possible by way of language to show logical form.

> In a certain sense we can talk about formal properties of objects and states of affairs, or, in the case of facts, about structural properties: and in the same sense about formal relations and structural relations. . . .
>
> It is impossible, however, to assert by means of propositions that such internal properties and relations exist: rather, they make themselves manifest in the propositions that represent the relevant states of affairs and are concerned with the relevant objects. (*T* 4.122)

However, what Wittgenstein suggests here does not help to understand the "propositions" of the *Tractatus*. The "logical properties of objects" are not shown by a special group of apparent propositions, say, those contained in the *Tractatus*. Rather, those properties are made manifest in "the propositions that represent the relevant states of affairs." But this seems to mean that only propositions that represent states of affairs can show logical form or any other logical property of objects. However, we have just seen that the "propositions" of the *Tractatus* do not and cannot represent any states of affairs.

This clearly exposes the perspective from which the *Tractatus* is written. It is as I have argued. Insofar as the "propositions" of the *Tractatus* are not "simply nonsense," they do speak from "outside the world." As we have already seen, it is precisely from there that the problem of the *Tractatus* arises, and so, of course, it is only from there that its solution can be articulated. The propositions of the *Tractatus* presuppose philosophical transcendence. Only for a subject who transcends the world and language could the *Tractatus* be intelligible. The doctrine of showing is designed to make such transcendence philosophically accessible without requiring a repudiation of the content of the *Tractatus*. To understand it, one must focus on what language shows, not on what is said. But to focus on what is shown is to take up the perspective of a transcendental subject—a subject that is "able to station [itself] . . . with propositions somewhere outside logic, that is to say outside the world." At the limit, language takes on a different role. It does not merely state or picture facts, it does something else—it shows or displays.

Elucidations

Apparently there is a way to use language that is not a matter of asserting facts, but that is still, "in a certain sense," talking about what cannot be said. Furthermore, this way of "talking about" is the way of the *Tractatus*, and it produces propositions that "serve as elucidations" (*T* 6.54). Philosophy, including the *Tractatus*, "consists essentially of elucidations" (*T* 4.112). But what is the nature of an elucidation? There are only three occurrences of that term in the *Tractatus*. In 4.112 Wittgenstein says that philosophy is not a body of doctrine but an activity that consists essentially in elucidations. Second, in the only passage in which he explicitly attends to the nature of an "elucidation," he says, "The meanings of primitive signs can be explained by means of elucidations. Elucidations are propositions that contain the primitive signs. So they can only be understood if the meanings of these signs are already known" (*T* 3.263). Finally, there is his statement that his "propositions serve as elucidations" (*T* 6.4).

It is noteworthy that two of these passages characterize philosophy as elucidation while the third uses that notion in connection with the problem of the meaning of primitive signs. Is "elucidation" the name for the entire activity of philosophy, or is its scope the more limited one of explaining primitive signs? Has Wittgenstein simply used the same term in connection with very different issues? That seems unlikely given the tight structure of the work. What, then, is the real connection between those apparently different issues?

Elucidations and Primitive Terms

To discover the connection, we begin with the only passage in which the notion of elucidations is itself the object of explanation, namely, *T* 3.263. "The meanings of primitive signs can be explained by means of elucidations. Elucidations are propositions that contain the primitive signs. So they can only be understood if the meanings of these signs are already known." Though this passage deals explicitly with the way in which the meaning of primitive signs is explained, there are parallels to the more general issue of the meaning of the "propositions" of the *Tractatus*. In both cases he calls attention to a peculiar role of language. In both cases there is a paradoxical quality involved. For elucidations as philosophy—the "propositions" of the

Tractatus—one must come to see what they "show" before they can be recognized as nonsensical, as not open to being understood. For elucidations as meaning, one must know what the terms to be explained by the elucidation mean before they can be understood.

One might be tempted to treat elucidation as a kind of ostensive definition, but that would be to seriously misread Wittgenstein. Typically, ostensive definitions occur independently of and preparatory to assertions and require us to suppose that words can appear in two different roles: in propositions and by themselves. Wittgenstein explicitly denies that possibility because it totally ignores his view that only in a proposition does a name have a meaning (T 3.3). To say that a given sign is the name of a particular object is to say that the sign meaningfully enters into a particular range of elementary propositions. Similarly, for an object to be the object that it is, at least in terms of form, is for it to be a constituent in a possible range of facts. Hence, what the referent of a given primitive term is, is necessarily tied up with the meaningful occurrence of that term in propositions. The relation here is internal, and the notion of ostensive definition simply ignores that. It makes no sense to suppose that we can first be acquainted with a simple object and then discover in which facts it is a possible constituent. This is precisely what is overlooked by the assimilation of elucidations to ostensive definitions.

There is, however, also something correct in that comparison. The rules governing the range of meaningful occurrences for a simple sign reflect the possible structure of facts. For a term to name an object, its linguistic behavior must mirror the behavior of the object. It is because objects enter into a given range of facts that their representatives, names, behave linguistically as they do. Conversely, it is because a given term behaves as it does that it is the name of the object that it names. Elucidation therefore presupposes prior acquaintance with the logical form of facts; the task at hand is to correlate terms with items in that structure. This is the way in which the comparison of elucidations with ostensive definitions is helpful.

If an elucidation is a proposition, it must exhibit the general form of a proposition. It must say: This is how things stand. To understand a proposition is to know how things stand if it is true. But to know that, one must already know what its terms mean, otherwise one will not know what fact is being pictured. Thus, insofar as we understand "elucidations" in terms of what they *say*, they necessarily fail as elucidations for they presuppose what they are to accomplish —an explanation of the meaning of terms.

The paradoxical character of elucidations arises precisely from the attempt to treat them exclusively in terms of a fact-stating function. But when we recognize that they play a radically different role, we properly understand them and avoid the difficulty apparently associated with them. Wittgenstein comments on this very difficulty in *Philosophical Remarks*. He says,

> If I explain the meaning of a word 'A' to someone by pointing to something and saying 'This is A', then this expression may be meant in two different ways. Either it is itself a proposition already in which case it can only be understood once the meaning of 'A' is known, i.e. I must now leave it to chance whether he takes it as I meant it or not. Or the sentence is a definition. Suppose I have said to someone 'A is ill', but he doesn't know who I mean by 'A', and I now point at a man, saying 'This is A'. Here the expression is a definition, but this can only be understood if he has gathered what kind of object it is through his understanding of the grammar of the proposition 'A is ill' . . . . And that of course is just another way of saying: I cannot use language to get outside language. (*PR* p. 54, section 6)

If "This is *A*" is to succeed in its role as "definition," the hearer must have already "gathered what kind of object" *A* is. In Tractarian language this means that one must have grasped the logical form that is shown by "*A* is ill." In this way a place is prepared for the use of "This is *A*" as a definition, and therefore it can bring the hearer to be aware of an object as the bearer of that name. This interplay between what is said and what is shown allows elucidations to achieve their purpose.

There are three passages that will help round out the issues here.

A proposition shows its sense.
A proposition shows how things stand if it is true. And says that they do so stand. (T 4.022)

The meanings of simple signs (words) must be explained to us if we are to understand them. (T 4.026)

What can be shown, cannot be said. (T 4.1212)

Why does Wittgenstein say that the meaning of simple signs must be explained? He is calling attention to a fundamental difference between propositions and names. It is essential to a proposition that "it should be able to communicate a new sense to us" (T 4.027). We need have no prior acquaintance with the state of affairs that is represented by it in order to understand it. If this were not so, only true propositions could be meaningful. So, as Wittgenstein says, "a proposition must use old expressions to communicate a new sense" (T 4.03). Thus, although the meaning of simple signs (old expressions) must be explained, the meaning of propositions need not be.

Now elucidations *show* what a primitive term means. Elucidations literally exhibit—are examples of—what they mean. How is this possible? Here the doctrine of logical form is critical. What a proposition has in common with the fact that it pictures is logical form. In virtue of that form it pictures what it does—the state of affairs is "put into words." The proposition is an instance of the same form or structure present in the state of affairs it represents. But the elements of the state of affairs, the objects, are not constituents of the linguistic instance of that form.

An analogy with an ordinary picture is helpful here. A picture taken as a picture (and not a play of colors and shapes, for example) is an *instance* of the structure of things that it pictures; it shows or exhibits that structure. To see a picture as a picture, one must see a set of colors and shapes as an instance of a structure. The picture shows what it pictures by being itself an instance of it.

To grasp a set of marks as a proposition is to see it in terms of its "projective relation" to a fact—as having logical form in common with that fact. To be acquainted with a set of marks as a proposition is to be acquainted with an instance of logical form as logical form. But, to repeat a critical point, naming (the way in which primitive signs mean) and logical form are not independent of each other. Again, the analogy with an ordinary picture is helpful. A particular spot of red in a picture is the sun only because of the relation that spot has to the other elements in the picture. Since the meaning of simple signs must be explained and since that can be done only via propositions and since a proposition must show its sense, Wittgenstein's paradox of elucidations—that elucidations explain the meaning of primitive signs but can be understood only if the meanings are already known—arises by ignoring the injunction that what can be shown cannot be said. It arises by treating the proposition in question in terms of what it says and not what it shows. At the same time it is important to keep before us the fact that it is in virtue of a proposition's saying *something* that it shows anything.

In fact, the account of showing developed here provides a clear explanation of why showing is something that only genuine propositions do. A proposition shows by being an instance of logical form, that is, by being a picture of an actual or possible state of affairs. As Wittgenstein puts it, a proposition shows its sense. But if this is correct, again we are confronted with the difficulty of giving an account of the *Tractatus* itself. Since its "propositions" are by its own standards not genuine, they can show nothing. Thus the doctrine fails to give us any help in understanding the work itself.

The function of an elucidation is to explain the meaning of a sign, and this is done by exhibiting the structure that depends on the naming relation between primitive sign and object. As we have seen, it is in virtue of that naming that all saying is possible. So elucidations are not a special class of propositions. Every genuine proposition both shows and says (*T* 4.022). They are simply "propositions that contain the primitive signs," but in treating them as elucidations, we attend to what they show and not to what they say. To talk about "explaining the meaning" of a term presupposes that the term has a meaning. It is only because "chair" means what it does that we can explain its meaning to someone. At this level explanations of meaning are only of psychological interest. They have no central place in a logical or philosophical account of meaning. That is, elucidations presuppose the meaningfulness of language and therefore cannot be part of an account of how meaning is possible.

Philosophy and Elucidations

We turn now to those passages in which philosophy is characterized as an activity that produces elucidations. Wittgenstein certainly is not saying merely that what is important about philosophy is the doing of it, not its results. This would be analogous to claiming that what is important about Latin is the process of studying it, not the Latin learned. This analogy, however, leaves untouched the notion that there are distinctively "philosophical propositions." Recall that if we take seriously the suggestion of 4.122 discussed earlier, logical form is not shown by special philosophical propositions but by ordinary nonphilosophical ones. The analogy with the study of Latin does not seem to capture this feature.

A more radical thesis would be that the results of philosophizing are themselves nonpropositional. Wittgenstein says, "Philosophy does not result in 'philosophical propositions', but rather in the clarification of propositions" (*T* 4.112).

There are at least two ways to develop the view of philosophy as clarification, and each involves the kind of transcendence of the world and language required by the doctrine of showing. We must focus either on what Wittgenstein does in the *Tractatus* or on what he says ought to be done. On the first alternative, the *Tractatus* itself will be taken as the paradigm of philosophy and its "propositions" as the sorts of clarifying elucidations mentioned above. This is what Wittgenstein suggests at 6.54 by saying that the propositions of the *Tractatus* are themselves elucidations. They do not "say" anything, but they do call attention to what is "shown" by there being any saying at all. To see that is to see that the "propositions" of the *Tractatus* are nonsensical. However, on this interpretation, the assertions of the *Tractatus* must be assigned a distinctive role. They do not show in the way that ordinary propositions do—in virtue of representing facts. Rather, they direct our attention to what can be seen only from "outside the world," which is what is common to both language and world. This leads directly to the transcendence that I have identified as presupposed both by the problems of the *Tractatus* and their solution. Showing provides philosophical access to the transcendent.

On the second alternative, we can focus on what Wittgenstein says would really count as proper philosophy, although it certainly is not what happens in the *Tractatus* itself.

> The correct method in philosophy would really be the following: to say nothing except what can be said, i.e. propositions of natural science—i.e. something that has nothing to do with philosophy—and then, whenever someone else wanted to say something metaphysical to demonstrate to him that he had failed to give a meaning to certain signs in his propositions. Although it would not be satisfying to the other person —he would not have the feeling that we were teaching him philosophy—this method would be the only strictly correct one. (*T* 6.53)

On this view, what has been done in the *Tractatus* is not philosophy. Philosophy is a totally negative enterprise that neither says nor shows anything. Rather, it guards against attempts to say what cannot be said: metaphysics. Philosophy per se does not deal in the transcendence of the *Tractatus*. It contents itself with a critical, corrective role.

This is the natural line suggested at 4.112.

Philosophy does not result in 'philosophical propositions', but rather in the clarification of propositions.

Without philosophy thoughts are, as it were, cloudy and indistinct: its task is to make them clear and to give them sharp boundaries.

What are the propositions that philosophy is to clarify? They are the propositions of natural science, which alone are "what can be said" (*T* 4.11, 4.113, 6.53).

Note that when Wittgenstein says that the totality of *true* propositions is the whole of natural science (*T* 4.11) and that what can be said are the propositions of natural science (*T* 6.53), he does not mean that false scientific propositions cannot be said! In 4.11 Wittgenstein is using the term "natural science" to refer to the outcome of ideal successful scientific inquiry. What would be left at the end of such inquiry is "the totality of true propositions." However, at 6.53, when Wittgenstein refers to "the propositions of natural science," he means to include all genuine propositions, true or false. Philosophy's task is to *clarify* the propositions of natural science, true or false, since, of course, philosophy has no way of its own to determine their truth. The results of such an activity, however, are clear "scientific propositions" and not philosophical propositions.

This alternative does not escape the need for transcendence, however, for although philosophy itself would not be a matter of the kind of showing that is in the *Tractatus*, "the correct method" could be justifiably taken as correct only by someone who has understood the "elucidations" of the *Tractatus*. This means that even if the *Tractatus* does not count as philosophy, it is a necessary prolegomenon. What it directs our attention to must be understood if the "correct method" is to be seen as correct. Without the *Tractatus*, the method of philosophy hangs in the air without justification. That is why someone subjected to this method without the "vision of the *Tractatus*" would not find it "satisfying."

There is also a second point. By what standard will one judge the clarity of propositions? Only if standards are presupposed can the "clarifying activity" of philosophy be motivated and evaluated. But standards cannot be generated by the activity itself. Rather, it is the vision of the *Tractatus*—including the notions of the totality of facts, elementary propositions, and objects—that provides the essential background against which the concept of "clarity" is given content. The *Tractatus* taken on its "positive" side is presupposed.

Philosophizing, therefore, is a kind of showing that goes beyond the showing of genuine propositions, or it presupposes such a showing. In either case, it requires language to play a role beyond that explicitly described in the *Tractatus*. It presupposes a role for language by means of which that which makes meaningful saying possible becomes philosophically accessible. This means that it presupposes a role for language in which it does not merely picture facts in the world but in which it speaks from beyond the world *and* language about the essential relations between the two. The doctrine of showing as what the *Tractatus* does gives us access to a perspective in which both the world and language are transcended. That perspective is precisely the perspective from which the *Tractatus* is written. It is the perspective of what Wittgenstein calls the "metaphysical subject." (See *T* 5.6 to 5.641.) By showing what makes language possible, we can give a non-language-bound articulation of the relation between language and the world and so provide a solution to the problem of meaning in the *Tractatus*.

Perhaps it would be useful to summarize where we have come. By distinguishing between saying and showing, Wittgenstein hopes to give an account of how the perspective from which the *Tractatus* is written can be present in language without being said therein. Unfortunately, this distinction does not help us to understand the sentences of the *Tractatus* itself because Wittgenstein contends that what a sentence shows it shows in virtue of what it says, but the sentences of the *Tractatus* say nothing. This led us to focus on Wittgenstein's claim that there are no "philosophical propositions" and to examine two alternative ways to understand the claim that philosophy is a matter of elucidations, but that each attempt presupposes transcendence that is made philosophically accessible by a showing that the sentences of the *Tractatus* provide. There seems to be no way to understand the *Tractatus* within the limits that the work sets out.

One representative attempt to avoid the charge that the *Tractatus* is methodologically incoherent is put forward by Max Black.[1] Black argues that Wittgenstein is simply too sweeping when he condemns his own work at the end of the *Tractatus*. It is true, he says, that the propositions of the *Tractatus* cannot say anything since they do not picture any facts, but it does not follow that they are meaningless gibberish. How can this be? Black calls attention to the fact that "sense" has two opposites in the *Tractatus*, only one of which is literal nonsense. The other meaning can be seen in tautologies. Tautologies lack sense, but it is not true that they are nonsense. That is, although tautologies do not picture any facts, they do something nonetheless. Tautologies are the essential by-products of any symbolism, but they convey no information. Rather, they show the structure of the method of representation. Thus tautologies provide us with an example of sentences that lack sense but are not nonsense.

Now, if tautologies express the "rules" of the symbolism, then many of the claims in the *Tractatus* can be seen as attempts to show aspects of logical symbolism. As Black puts it,

This line of defense applies to all cases in which Wittgenstein is seeking the 'essence' of something. In all such cases, his investigation, whether successful or not, results in an *a priori* statement that ought to be treated, on his principles, as the expression of a certain rule.[2]

Thus, much of the *Tractatus* can be saved, for it will consist in attempts to make clear the rules of our language, not, of course, of English or German, but of any adequate vehicle of representation. Wittgenstein is attempting to set out the rules for any possible language, not merely the grammatical rules of some particular language.

Exactly what cases would count as ones in which Wittgenstein is seeking the "essence" of something? Consider, for example, the claim that the general form (essence?) of a proposition is: This is how things stand (T 4.5). It would certainly be natural to say that Wittgenstein was here expressing the essence of language, yet it does not seem possible to suppose that this is a tautology or a covert rule. This contention about the general form of a proposition is clearly connected with Wittgenstein's view that the world is the totality of facts and with the whole picture theory. This generates a serious difficulty for Black's defense.

Black is very clear that the defense he offers cannot be applied to all the "claims" of the *Tractatus*. In fact, he admits that it cannot be applied to the "most striking," apparently metaphysical claims such as "The world is the totality of facts, not of things."[3] These cannot be seen as covert tautologies. Herein lies the problem. Wittgenstein's account of tautologies is not independent of his account of meaning, and that account is necessarily tied to the metaphysical assertions of the *Tractatus*. Wittgenstein's argument concerning the status of necessary truths depends on his picture theory of meaning. Since every picture must be distinct from the state of affairs that it pictures, each can vary independently of the other, and this means that there can be no necessarily true pictures. Thus, propositions that appear to be pictures but are necessarily true must not be genuine pictures or propositions at all. So the "rule" account of necessary truths is forced on Wittgenstein by the account of meaning that is required by his conception of the world as the totality of facts. This means that Black's attempt to save the *Tractatus* can be accepted only if he can also give an account of the "most striking" assertions in it. Let us therefore turn to what he says there.

Black thinks it is possible both to admit that "many of the most interesting of the [*Tractatus*'] statements must indeed be treated as 'nonsensical'"[4] and at the same time to contend that "these statements can have important uses." Is this a real possibility? Consider, for example, "The world is the totality of facts" or "The general form of a proposition is: This is how things stand" (both of which actually express the same idea). Suppose we take seriously the idea that these are strictly nonsense because they attempt to say what can only be shown. In what would such a showing consist? One suggestion is perhaps supported by Wittgenstein's proposal that "the correct method would really be the following: to say nothing except what can be said, i.e. the propositions of natural science" (*T* 6.53). That the world is the totality of facts would be shown by a review of meaningful assertions, all of which express some fact. In this way the limits of language show that the world is the totality of facts without saying it. The *Tractatus* then might be viewed as Wittgenstein's attempt to get us to see what the language shows. Even though its claims are nonsensical, they have a role to play.

This proposal will not work for reasons similar to those given earlier in regard to Wittgenstein's suggestion that we can "set the limits of language" by working our way out from the inside, thus avoiding the necessity to "think both sides of the limit." The problem, simply put, is that the claim in question—"The general form of a proposition is: This is how things stand"—functions to set the limit by means of which the class of meaningful propositions is determined. However, the proposal developed above treats it as though it were a member of that class. We could follow that suggestion only if we already had an independent standard of meaningfulness, that is, some standard to delimit the class of meaningful assertions. Then that class, so delimited, might "show" that the world is the totality of facts. But, of course, we do not have any such standard. If, as seems a more likely procedure, we begin with some "pre-theoretical intuitions" about what is meaningful, it is very probable that controversy will break out precisely over whether or not to include among the class of meaningful assertions some that might be taken to "show" that the limits of meaningful discourse and empirical fact do not coincide.

All of this is to say that one cannot avoid the metaphysics of the *Tractatus* by appealing to its theory of language because that theory presupposes the metaphysics. What this means is that if we allow such claims—the metaphysical assertions of the *Tractatus*—to "turn out to be nonsense" as Black suggests, we will no longer have any reason for supposing that they are nonsense. And we cannot justify both the metaphysics and the theory of language by an appeal to our intuitions about meaning. Perhaps Wittgenstein thought that he could do that, but if so, he simply based his intuitions on "too narrow a diet of examples" (to borrow a phrase from the later philosophy).

Perhaps all the problems with understanding the *Tractatus* can be avoided by simply granting that in a sense the work itself is unnecessary. If the logic of our language were perspicuous, the limits of language would be clear. As Wittgenstein says, "once we have a sign-language in which everything is all right, we already have a correct logical point of view" (*T* 4.1213). Since we do not have such a language, we (philosophers) have to say things in the attempt to attain a perspicuous view. The things we say are really nonsensical, but we say them because they direct attention to the implicit limits of language. In this way philosophizing is a necessary corrective for our failure to see the limits of our language. The *Tractatus* serves that function. (And, after all, isn't that what Wittgenstein had in mind with the famous ladder metaphor at the end of the *Tractatus*?) At 6.54 Wittgenstein says, "anyone who understands *me* eventually recognizes *them* [the propositions of the *Tractatus*] as nonsense" (my emphasis). Understanding the *Tractatus* is not a matter of grasping the meaning of certain philosophical propositions. Rather, it is a matter of understanding what Wittgenstein is *doing*. And, of course, he may successfully do that even by uttering or writing nonsense sentences. In fact, anyone who is led to a "correct logical point of view" by Wittgenstein's Tractarian comments will "throw away the ladder after he has climbed up it" (*T* 6.54).

Perhaps such an account accurately represents Wittgenstein's self-understanding, but it does not escape the criticism developed here. By what standard are we to recognize a "sign-language in which everything is all right?" Isn't such a language one that meets the conditions set out in the *Tractatus*? Then we must be able to understand what those conditions are. That is, we must understand the various "claims" about language and its relation to the world that we have been focused on, the truth of which is "unassailable." Perhaps it is true that were the logic of our language "perspicuous," the *Tractatus* would be unnecessary but only because our language would already allow us to see exactly what the *Tractatus* brings us to see. And it is this seeing of certain things that the language of the *Tractatus* brings about by its *showing*. But the things we see by way of the language of the *Tractatus* are not facts in the world but the unutterable and necessary conditions that bind language to the world. And we see them by standing "outside logic, that is to say outside the world" (*T* 4.12). Thus, Wittgenstein still must make philosophically accessible a transcendence that cannot be said, and he must do it using language.

Comparisons

The similarities between philosophical elucidations and elucidations of meaning are obvious. Metaphysicians have seen the attempt to articulate the conditions for the possibility of meaning as attempts to picture a special order of facts: necessary facts. As such, their claims transgress the very conditions that give them meaning. It is necessary to recognize the unique role that language plays at this juncture. If one seeks a positive characterization for elucidations, it might be appropriate to call them "linguistic" or "grammatical remarks" that explain or establish the meaning of terms. The confusion of these grammatical remarks with factual claims, fostered by the essential interdependence of showing and saying, generates the problems that are solved by calling attention to their deeper differences. Again, elucidations are not a special class of propositions that speak about a special range of facts. They are merely ordinary propositions attended to with reference to what they show.

Here we have in capsule form themes concerning the practice of philosophy common both to the early and later writings. It is no accident that Wittgenstein sees his own philosophical remarks as elucidations in the sense developed here. It is truly ironic that we discover that Wittgenstein's picture theory of meaning is itself incomplete without the recognition that language cannot picture unless it has another role, a role in which it "does something"—namely, show. Implicit in the *Tractatus* in a highly restricted form is one of the central insights of the later philosophy. As we shall see, it is limited in the way the whole *Tractatus* is—it places such doing outside the world, not with particular situated selves, but with a "philosophical self."

Elucidations involve a role for language that does not fall under the account of meaning given in the *Tractatus*. This role becomes apparent only at the limit. So long as we stay within the sphere of language, saying only what can be said, its capacity to show does not become apparent. It is only when we are tempted to raise certain questions and say what cannot be said that we must be shown the error of our ways. Elucidations of meaning direct attention to objects and to the relation of those objects to the very language employed. The possibility of stating facts rests on the philosophical success of the elucidation. At the same time, a proposition's role as an elucidation presupposes its fact-stating capacity. Language states only because it shows, and it shows only because it states.

Unfortunately, the account developed here still does not allow one to understand the sentences of the *Tractatus* themselves. If showing and saying are essentially interdependent, then only sentences that say, that is, picture some fact, can show, but the sentences of the *Tractatus* do not picture any fact. Rather, they are meant to direct our attention to the conditions for the possibility of meaning. This showing makes philosophically accessible the transcendence that gives the whole work its unique perspective and that is embodied in Wittgenstein's view of the "metaphysical subject" discussed in 5.6 to 5.641. Of course, this transcendence is also rejected by the explicit doctrines and recommended methods of the *Tractatus*.

4

THE METAPHYSICAL SUBJECT

The various lines of inquiry we have examined have all led to the showing/saying distinction. Not only is that distinction necessary for a full explication of the logical doctrine of objects that underlies the whole picture theory, it is also required to understand the nature of the so-called elucidations contained in the *Tractatus*. Wittgenstein's elucidations seem to be designed to call attention to what language shows. Since, however, what can be shown cannot be said (*T* 4.1212), his claims cannot say what language shows. Still, they do somehow give linguistic expression to it. The showing/saying distinction is, therefore, not merely a special doctrine developed in the *Tractatus* (of course it is that), but more importantly the work itself can be understood only in terms of showing. The doctrine of showing is contained in the work and also is the medium through which the work is expressed. Wittgenstein, himself, says of the *Tractatus*:

> The main point is the theory of what can be expressed (gasagt) by prop[ositions]—i.e. by language—(and what comes to the same thing what can be thought) and what can not be expressed by prop[osition]s, but only shown (gezeigt); which, I believe, is the cardinal problem of philosophy. (*RKM* R. 37, p. 71)

Implicit in the distinction and in the attempt to give expression to what is shown is the notion of a standpoint "somewhere outside logic, that is outside the world" (*T* 4.12) from which we gain access to the problems and language of the *Tractatus*. Wittgenstein's discussion of the metaphysical subject in 5.6 to 5.641 attends explicitly to such a standpoint.

Why does Wittgenstein feel it necessary to introduce a metaphysical subject into what otherwise appears to be a rigorous and unrelenting realism? The answer has to do with representation: if one fact (a sentence) is to represent another fact (a state of affairs), there must be a subject. A fact merely as a state of affairs and a fact as a representing sentence are logically distinct. Only for a subject can one fact represent another. Without subjectivity there would be merely an unarticulated totality of facts. Thus subjectivity is a *logically* necessary condition for the possibility of representation. However, because the *Tractatus* is concerned with representation as such, not with particular forms of representation, the subjectivity required is in no sense particular. Rather, it is the totality of facts *as* representable. Therefore, the metaphysical subject cannot be an item in the world, but the limit of the world considered as the limit of all possible representation. As we shall see, this distinction between the metaphysical subject and a particular individual subject lies at the center of Wittgenstein's treatment of solipsism.

Wittgenstein begins his discussion of subjectivity with the contention that "*the limits of my language* mean the limits of my world" (*T* 5.6) and ends with a characterization of the philosophical self. "The philosophical self is not the human being, not the human body, or the human soul, with which psychology deals, but rather the metaphysical subject, the limit of the world—not a part of it" (*T* 5.641). This is an especially dense and difficult part of the *Tractatus*, and a careful reading of it is essential to a full understanding of the work.

In the first place, there is a baffling array of terms implying subjectivity that figure in these few sections. Wittgenstein talks about "my world," "the subject," "the metaphysical subject," "the self of solipsism," "the philosophical self," "the human being" including both "the human body" and "the human soul." In this diversity there are, in fact, two distinct notions of subjectivity, which I will call "the empirical subject" and, following Wittgenstein, "the metaphysical subject." In order to give a full account of the *Tractatus*, it will be necessary to introduce a third notion, the willing subject, but this is not discussed in these passages. Rather, it plays a central role in the ethical dimensions of the *Tractatus*, which will be developed later. The empirical subject is for Wittgenstein the human being, the human body and soul, which is relegated to psychology and so is of no interest to philosophy. On the other hand, the metaphysical subject, which is also called "the philosophical self," is the self insofar as it can be talked about nonpsychologically *in philosophy*. It is the self for which the world is "my world." Of course, the empirical subject can also be talked about, but there is nothing that philosophy as such can say. Since Wittgenstein clearly identifies the metaphysical subject and the philosophical self, I propose to use the term "metaphysical subject" throughout the discussion of this chapter to refer to that subjectivity which can be talked about by philosophy and which is discussed in 5.6 to 5.641. In this chapter the focus will be on the metaphysical subject in relation to the empirical subject. In later chapters, after the ethical aspects have been presented, all three notions of subjectivity will be examined in their interrelation.

The Empirical Subject

What is the difference between the empirical and the metaphysical subject? This can best be answered by dealing with the problem of intentional terms in relation to Wittgenstein's thesis of extensionality. The empirical subject—the human being, the human body, even the human soul—is an item in the world along with other items. Its nature, behavior, and character are open to empirical investigation—nothing more and nothing less—and the result of such investigations "has nothing to do with philosophy" (T 6.53). But the idea that particular, individual selves constitute special philosophical problems derives in part from confusions surrounding propositions containing intentional terms such as "believes" or "hopes." Such sentences do not appear to fit Wittgenstein's analysis because they contain a proposition as a component. For example, "Hodges believes that the Sounds won the game" contains the propositional component "The Sounds won the game." But it is not a truth function of its components.

At 5.54 Wittgenstein says, "In the general propositional form propositions occur in other propositions only as bases of truth-operations." This is a version of "the thesis of extensionality"—the thesis that all complex propositions are truth functions of elementary propositions. On this view, the truth of any complex proposition must be completely and uniquely determined by the truth value of the component propositions, and the truth of each elementary proposition must be logically independent of every other. In light of this, what are we to say about "Hodges believes . . ."? If it is elementary, how can it have a propositional component? If it is complex, why isn't it a truth function of its components? And what sort of thing is Hodges that seems to stand in some kind of relation to the proposition?

Wittgenstein is aware of these obvious problems. He says,

> At first sight it looks as if it were also possible for one proposition to occur in another in a different way.
>
> Particularly with certain forms of proposition in psychology, such as 'A believes that p is the case' and 'A has the thought that p' etc.
>
> For if these are considered superficially, it looks as if the proposition p stood in some kind of relation to an object A. (T 5.541)

This apparent counterexample to the thesis of extensionality also seems to reveal a special sort of object, an object, A, that can stand in an intentional, nonconstitutive relation to an independently constituted fact, actual or possible. This object is a subject that is a necessary constituent in a range of mental facts that include other facts as their constituents.

Unfortunately, Wittgenstein's treatment of the problems raised here is by no means clear. Consider the passages in which he offers his solution.

> It is clear, however, that 'A believes that p' . . . [is] of the form ' "p" says p': and this does not involve a correlation of a fact with an object but rather the correlation of facts by means of the correlation of their objects.
>
> This shows too that there is no such thing as the soul—the subject, etc.—as it is conceived in the superficial psychology of the present day.
>
> Indeed a composite soul would no longer be a soul. (T 5.5421–5422)

There are two distinct issues under discussion in these sections. One is the thesis of extensionality and the other is the status of the believer. Both of these problems are addressed by Wittgenstein's claim that although the grammatical form of "A believes that p" suggests that the corresponding fact is a complex in which both A as believer and p as constituent occur, its actual form is " 'p' says p." But what can that possibly mean? What happened to A? A simply drops out of consideration because for a moment Wittgenstein is not focused on the problem of the status of the self but on the problem of intentionality, and that requires that the apparent intentional relation "believes" or "thinks" be eliminated and with it the nonextensional occurrence of p.

How is this to be done? If "A believes that p" is of the form " 'p'

says p," then, appearances to the contrary notwithstanding, it is not the case that there exists an intentional relation between A and an actual or possible fact. There is no violation of the thesis of extensionality because no proposition occurs within another nontruth functionally. In " 'p' says p" the first occurrence of p takes sentences as its values. Sentences, as here understood, are not intentional objects and thus do not stand in intentional relations. The intentionality is shifted to the relation between "p" and p and, as Wittgenstein says, "This does not involve a correlation of a fact with an object, but rather the correlation of facts by means of a correlation of their objects." "P" is a fact—every sentence is—and it is only because of that that it can "say" anything. This just is the Tractarian picture theory. To show that "p" says p is to specify the particular method of projection that correlates the elements or objects of "p" with those of p. The specifics of such a correlation are a matter for psychology to determine. Of course, the logical features of any such correlation —the very possibility of representation—are the subject matter of the *Tractatus* itself, but they are prior to any particular representation. Thus the "burden of intentionality" either evaporates into psychology or is carried by Wittgenstein's theory of meaning. In any case, "psychological sentences" constitute no special problem.

Of course, there is still a question about A and its relation to "p," but Wittgenstein does not see that as problematic for the obvious reason that whatever that relation is, it is not intentional. Specifically, we are not required to suppose that there is a simple object that stands in a nonconstitutive relation to an actual or possible fact. The proposition "A says p" would be analyzed along the following lines: "A uttered the sentence 'p' which says p." Obviously, this will not do as a complete analysis because it is possible for A to say p without uttering the sentence "p," but such subtleties are not at issue here. In fact, in a letter to Russell, responding to the question "Does a Gedanke [thought] consist of words?" Wittgenstein says "No! But of psychical constituents that have the same relation to reality as words" (*RKM* R. 37, p. 72). By saying that there are "psychical constituents," he seems to be supposing only a different medium of representation. But such differences are irrelevant to the issues of the *Tractatus*. "A gramophone record, the musical idea, the written notes, and the sound waves, all stand to one another in the same internal relation of depicting that holds between language and the world" (*T* 4.014). Of course, the differences here will be important for the psychology of representation, but that is a different enterprise.

Given this discussion, it should be clear that the Tractarian problem of meaning cannot be solved by an appeal to mental acts of meaning. What language and world must have in common, thought and world must also have in common. Although thoughts are not identical with sentences (any more than a musical score is identical with a recording), they both stand in the same "internal relation" to the world insofar as they represent. Neither can be used to account for the fact of meaning with regard to the other. Thought has no magical powers for Wittgenstein.

The only subject that we find in all this is one that has no special unity or simplicity. There is a subject that engages in linguistic behavior, that utters the sentence "*p*," and this is a subject open to empirical inquiry. As such, it is open to a variety of descriptions and characterizations, and so is "composite" in the Tractarian sense. Thus Wittgenstein says of the sort of analysis offered above, "This shows too that there is no such thing as the soul—the subject, etc. . . . Indeed a composite soul would no longer be a soul" (*T* 5.5421). The issue that has been before us is the status of the subject of such sentences as "*A* believes that *p*." But the analysis offered shows that *A* presents no philosophical problems. Its status is that of any other item investigated by science. It unity and identity similarly are not unique. The empirical self is not an object in the *Tractatus* sense and can lay no claim to metaphysical unity.

Wittgenstein's discussion is intended to show that there is nothing in common between the subject as it is studied by psychology and the subject required by the theory of representation in the *Tractatus*. The first is a specific sets of facts in the world. Such a self is an item (but not an "object" in the technical sense) in the world, not a condition for the possibility of representing the world. It is represented, pictured, or talked about. Though it may be of substantial interest to psychology, it is of no special philosophical interest. In fact, its only interest is derived from the propensity of philosophers to illicitly confuse such a situated empirical subject with the philosophical or metaphysical subject to produce the illusion of solipsism.

The Metaphysical Subject

Let us now turn directly to the metaphysical subject, beginning with Wittgenstein's claim that "*the limits of my language* mean the limits of my world" (*T* 5.6). In light of the previous discussion it should be clear that such limits are not psychological, personal, or individual. In fact, the limits of my language are precisely the limits it has, not in virtue of being mine, but in virtue of being language at all—in virtue of being a mode of representation. So the limits of the possibility of representation are simply the limits of the world, of what can be represented. Any representation is of a logically possible state of affairs, and any logically possible state of affairs is representable. "Logic pervades the world: the limits of the world are also its limits" (*T* 5.61). So the limits of the language by means of which I represent the world (my language) are the limits of the world that I represent (my world). The "I" and "my" here, however, refer not to an idiosyncratic individual—an item in the world—but to myself as representer pure and simple—the subject by which all representation qua representation occurs. Such a "pure representer" is not and cannot be an item in the world. It cannot be represented. "The subject does not belong to the world: Rather, it is a limit of the world. . . . Where in the world is a metaphysical subject to be found?" (*T* 5.632–633). This pure representer is the metaphysical subject.

This leads us immediately to the famous passages dealing with solipsism, 5.62 and 5.64. Wittgenstein says that 5.6 ("*The limits of my language* mean the limits of my world") provides the key to the problem of how much truth there is in solipsism.

> For what the solipsist means is quite correct; only it cannot be said but makes itself manifest. The world is my world: This is manifest in the fact that the limits of language (the only language that I understand) mean the limits of my world. (*T* 5.62)

Notice that I accept the Russell/Hintikka/Lewy translation[1] of the parenthetical expression in contrast to that offered by Pears and McGuinness in the translation referred to herein. The latter two translate the parenthetical expression as "of that language which alone I understand." Although the German will allow either translation, there are two points in favor of the former. First, the actual German is "der Sprache, die allein ich verstehe." If Wittgenstein had wanted to emphasize that only he understood the language, it would have been more customary to write "die ich allein," not "die allein ich." Second, the former more clearly conveys the essentially nonpersonal character meant here. The point of saying that it is the only language that I understand is that language is here being considered from a purely logical point of view. Therefore, this translation is to be preferred on both linguistic and philosophical grounds.

It could make no sense to suggest that although the limits of my language mean the limits of my world, this is not the case for you. There can be no relevant difference between your language and mine when both are being considered exclusively from the standpoint of the *Tractatus*—as modes of representation. In this sense every language must, as language, have the same limits as mine. Whatever differences might exist would be of interest only to psychology. So the world that I represent via language just is *the* world. The world is my world. This "truth of solipsism" is simply the necessary coincidence of the limits of representing and of the represented seen from the point of view of representation, that is, from the point of view of a pure representer. And of course, this is why "solipsism, when its implications are followed out strictly, coincides with pure realism. The self of solipsism shrinks to a point without extension and there remains the reality coordinate with it" (T 5.64). But what is coordinate with the self of solipsism is simply what is represented: the world. In the *Notebooks* Wittgenstein offers his own commentary on this passage. He says,

> This is the way I have travelled: Idealism singles men out from the world as unique, solipsism singles me alone out, and at last I see that I too belong with the rest of the world, and so on the one side *nothing* is left over, and on the other side, as unique, *the world*. In this way idealism leads to realism if it is strictly thought out. (*NB* p. 85, 15.10.16)

The "self of solipsism" is merely the possibility of representation, of language. But the general form of a proposition is: This is how things stand. Language says how things stand. So if we consider what can be said, we have the totality of facts or the world (T 1.1). That there is representation *shows* "the truth of solipsism." That is why Wittgenstein says in the famous comparison with the visual field that "nothing in the visual field allows you to infer that it is seen by an eye" (T 5.633). We become aware of that only by recognizing that it is a visual field. Similarly, "the truth of solipsism" cannot be inferred from anything that is represented but from the "fact" that it is represented. The metaphysical subject is language taken as the possibility of representation, and that is precisely the "sense in which philosophy can talk about the self in a non-psychological way" (T 5.641). Such talk is the task of the *Tractatus*.

The traditional solipsist begins with a particular self and "discovers" that everything occurs within its purview. Of course, this is strictly false if "its purview" means the actual purview of an individual. It becomes true only when we shift from talk about the actual experience of a particular self to possible experience. But this shift is ignored by the solipsist. In his proclamation that the world is his world, he continues to refer to himself as a particular item in the world and as the limit of the world. Wittgenstein overcomes that confusion by rigorously maintaining his distinction between what can be said and what can be shown. The self as sayable is an item in the world, not its limit; the self as shown by saying is the limit of the world, not an item in it.

The traditional solipsist, along with all metaphysicians, tries to say what can only be shown. What makes the solipsist's position so provocative is that he seems to be saying that what one takes, at first glance, to be an item within the order of the world—a particular situated empirical self—is, in fact, the limit of the world. By doing so the solipsist turns a logical insight about the limits of possible representation into a piece of philosophical nonsense that has the deceptive quality of the discovery of a surprising "fact." Wittgenstein, by carefully separating the two notions of subjectivity involved, can, at one and the same time, give us the "truth of solipsism" and dispel its provocative character.

The Unsayable and the Metaphysical Subject

It is critical to notice here a related point that Wittgenstein makes. "There *really is* a sense in which philosophy can *talk about* the self in a non-psychological way" (*T* 5.641, my emphasis). That is to say, there is a way in which language can be used to express the unsayable. The very possibility of the *Tractatus* depends on that. It calls attention to what language shows, to features that are the necessary conditions for the possibility of all representation. So the *Tractatus* speaks from and about the limit of both language and the world. In this sense the point of view of the *Tractatus* is the point of view of the metaphysical subject. Once again we see that the *Tractatus* is firmly committed to the belief that language can be used to present language and the world as a whole—from outside of language. The *Tractatus* itself is an instance of that. Of course, its methodological injunctions reject such a possibility, but for reasons that can be intelligible only if there is such a possibility. In this way the *Tractatus* both requires and rejects the transcendence of the metaphysical subject. For example, if we limit ourselves to what can be said, we cannot speak of the metaphysical subject. But if we cannot speak of that subject, we cannot speak of the limits of what can be said. It will not be possible for philosophy to talk about the self in a nonpsychological way.

The difficulties here are but a version of the fundamental paradox of the *Tractatus*, which we will confront later in another and, perhaps, more explicit form in relation to the ethical thinking. The problem can be put as follows. If the *Tractatus* is possible, then the perspective from which it is written must be capable of linguistic expression. But whatever is capable of such expression must be an item in the world (given the theory of representation in the *Tractatus*). As such, however, it can be only one among many possibilities, not the limit of all possibility. So if the *Tractatus* can be written, it cannot accomplish its purpose (to set the limits of all possible representation); and if it accomplishes its purpose, it cannot be written. We seem to be forced to treat subjectivity in the *Tractatus* both as an item in the world so that it can be talked about and transcendentally as a condition of the world. But this violates Wittgenstein's own insight in relation to the problem of solipsism. In short, Wittgenstein, himself, seems to be committed to the "self of solipsism" —an individual self that is, at the same time, treated as the limit of the world.

The propositions of the *Tractatus* are, by the very standards that they articulate, nonsensical.

My propositions serve as elucidations in the following way: anyone who understands me eventually recognizes them as nonsensical, when he has used them—as steps—to climb up beyond them. (He must, so to speak, throw away the ladder after he has climbed up it.) (*T* 6.5)

We saw earlier that the ladder metaphor cannot be explained so as to avoid problems here generated. Insofar as the *Tractatus* is intelligible, it violates its own stated limits. But if it is unintelligible, then the very limits it proposes and by which it is judged to be unintelligible are themselves unintelligible.

If the propositions of the *Tractatus* are nonsense, then the problem with which it begins is without an articulable solution. However, as we have already seen, the early Wittgenstein is perhaps never more explicit than in his rejection of the idea of a problem with no solution.

When the answer cannot be put into words, neither can the question be put into words.

The riddle does not exist.

If a question can be framed at all, it is also possible to answer it. (*T* 6.5)

It is as though Wittgenstein has allowed himself to speak nonsense in order to put an end to nonsense. But strictly speaking, "What we cannot speak about we must pass over in silence" (*T* 7). The *Tractatus* cannot be written.

5

THE ETHICAL

The tensions identified on the logical side of the *Tractatus* become even more acute as we turn to the ethical. The ethical side of the *Tractatus* is not a mere unimportant addendum to a work primarily focused on other issues. Although discussion of ethics occupies a relatively small portion, Wittgenstein indicates that the whole point of the *Tractatus* is ethical.[1] Of course, this does not imply that the logical dimensions of the *Tractatus* are not of great importance to Wittgenstein. Certainly they are. However, let me remind you of what Engelmann said in comparing Wittgenstein to the Positivists,

> He has something of enormous importance in common with the positivists; he draws the line between what we can speak about and what we must be silent about just as they do. The difference is only that they have nothing to be silent about. Positivism holds—and this is its essence—that what we can speak about is all that matters in life. *Whereas Wittgenstein passionately believes that all that really matters in life is precisely what, in his view, we must be silent about.* When he nevertheless takes immense pains to delimit the unimportant, it is not the coastline of that island which he is bent on surveying with such meticulous accuracy, but the boundary of the ocean. (*LLW* p. 97)

On this view the logical structure developed in the *Tractatus* is for the sake of an ethical vision. And this means that the ethical dimension of his early thought must be taken with complete seriousness and placed at the center of his philosophy. If this is to be done, the limited materials of the *Tractatus* proper must be supplemented by the *Notebooks* and the "Lecture on Ethics."

Perhaps some justification is required for the use of the *Notebooks* in developing an interpretation of Wittgenstein's ethical views. After all, he did not intend that the work be published. It could be argued that what he wanted from the *Notebooks* is to be found in the *Tractatus* and what is left in the *Notebooks* should be taken to be what Wittgenstein wanted to be silent about. On this account the ethical materials that are in the *Notebooks* but not included in the *Tractatus* are excluded for explicit philosophical reasons. It is the stated view of the *Tractatus* that ethics cannot be put into words (*T* 6.421). So what was "put into words" in the *Notebooks* must be excluded from the rigorous presentation of Wittgenstein's philosophy that occurs in the *Tractatus*.

Certainly this argument has some force. It would be a mistake to argue that Wittgenstein really held a certain view because it is found in the *Notebooks* but rejected or modified in the *Tractatus*. Wherever there is an explicit difference between the two, the *Tractatus* must be taken as definitive. However, that is not the situation with the ethical reflections. There is no contradiction or modification of views from the one to the other. Rather, the *Notebooks* simply contain a great deal more discussion of the same claims made in the *Tractatus*. When this discussion is taken in conjunction with the very brief and compact entries of the *Tractatus*, the *Notebooks* deepen and amplify its claims. It is not that what we find in the *Notebooks* requires us to change our view about what Wittgenstein says in the *Tractatus*. Rather, it allows us to carry the interpretation to a much deeper level.

That Wittgenstein did not feel it necessary to remain literally silent on ethical matters is also clear from the "Lecture on Ethics," which he gave in 1929 or 1930 but which was not published until 1965.

As we shall see, that work continues Tractarian themes and sheds substantial light on the structure of Wittgenstein's ethical thought. There is a second point that needs to be made. We have already argued that the whole body of the *Tractatus* violates its own criteria for what can be said. And Wittgenstein is aware of that himself. The point is simply that, for example, "Objects are simple" (*T* 2.02) is also not sayable in the Tractarian account and for the same reasons that ethics is not. So it seems clear that Wittgenstein did not exclude the ethical remarks of the *Notebooks* because they are unsayable. Had Wittgenstein refused, quite literally, to say what is unsayable, he would not have written the *Tractatus* at all.

Finally, if the interpreter of Wittgenstein ignores the materials of the *Notebooks*, he or she simply ignores a major source of this thought that, as we shall see, casts substantial light on the larger philosophical and historical setting in which the *Tractatus* is to be understood. For these reasons I will make liberal use of the *Notebooks*, never to contradict claims found in the *Tractatus* but to extend our understanding of them.

The major contention here is that both the unity and transcendence of the philosophical self, so essential to Wittgenstein's treatment of solipsism, are radically compromised by his ethical vision. In fact, to take his ethical views seriously is either to reintroduce solipsism in its most *metaphysical* form or it is to compromise totally the purity of the transcendental perspective from which the *Tractatus* is written.

The points to be made concerning the ethical subject are really quite simple. The ethical subject must transcend the world in the way that the metaphysical subject does, for "ethics is transcendental" (*T* 6.421). However, the ethical subject must also be individual —a subject among other subjects—if the good life is achievable. In the end it is I, Michael Hodges, who attains or fails to attain the good life. But this combination reveals the same ambiguity in the ethical subject that was discovered on the logical side in the previous chapter. That is, it involves confusing the metaphysical subject, or in this case the ethical subject, with a particular empirical self. Remember that the metaphysical subject is simply language taken in its representing capacity. There is no room here for the notion of an "individual subject." The attempt to think about the metaphysical subject as a particular self is the very heart of solipsism understood as a theory, and it is this that Wittgenstein rejects by way of his own account of philosophical subjectivity as language. However, that is compromised both by his own attempt to give voice to such a view in the *Tractatus* itself and now by his treatment of the ethical subject. The ethical subject both transcends the world—in order for it to be ethical at all—and it is in the world as one subject among others—in order for the good life to be achievable. But now a subject that is both individual and at the limit of the world yields a solipsism in which the self does not shrink to a point without extension, and this precisely is the solipsism that Wittgenstein was trying to avoid.

If, in order to avoid this resurgent solipsism, Wittgenstein were to relativize "ethical transcendence" by treating it as a particular attitude that an empirical subject might take to the world, there would be two results. First, for ethical theory itself, it would undermine the status of ethical value by "bringing it into the world." Second, the door would be opened to treating "metaphysical transcendence" in the same way. On this option, which, I contend, the later Wittgenstein actually develops, the so-called limits of the world would merely be the limits of a *particular* way of representing the world—one way among others. What this would mean is that the perspective from which the *Tractatus* is written, that of the metaphysical subject, could no longer claim to be strictly and absolutely transcendental. Thus the "claims" of the work would no longer represent *the* limits of all possible representation. In fact, without such an absolute perspective, the very notions of "all possible representation" and "the totality of facts," and so forth, would dissolve.

Actually this is a fascinating result for the project of this book, for what it shows is that the very act of writing the *Tractatus*—representing the limits of all possible representation—when consistently thought through propels one in the direction of the later philosophy in which the very terms of the Tractarian project can no longer be given the necessary meaning.

At the moment, however, what all of this shows is that something must give: either Wittgenstein's "refutation of solipsism" and with it his project to set the a priori "limits to all possible representation" or his account of the ethical. In fact, matters are not even that straightforward since, as we have already seen, even the treatment of the metaphysical subject, taken on its own terms, already contains the fundamental ambiguity concerning subjectivity, which it is designed to overcome. In any case, however, as we shall see, the ethical and the logical are so closely tied together that it is not possible merely to "give up" one or the other. If either goes, all the issues of the *Tractatus* will be radically transformed.

The Status of the Ethical

In an interesting but little discussed passage toward the end of the *Tractatus* Wittgenstein says,

> The whole modern conception of the world is founded on the illusion that the so-called laws of nature are the explanations of natural phenomena.
>
> Thus people today stop at the laws of nature, treating them as something inviolable, just as God and Fate were treated in past ages.
>
> And in fact both are right and both wrong: though the view of the ancients is clearer in so far as they have a clear and acknowledged terminus, while the modern system tries to make it look as if *everything* were explained. (*T* 6.371–372)

This is the transition from the purely logical elements of the *Tractatus* to the so-called ethical/mystical sections. Wittgenstein finds neither the "modern conception" nor the "view of the ancients" adequate, but for different reasons. Understanding how they both fail makes room for Wittgenstein's own treatment of what is "higher."

The key here is in the notion of "explanation." Max Black contends that Wittgenstein's attitude "toward the concept of explanation is distinctly unsympathetic." [2] But this is to miss the whole point. Wittgenstein is not rejecting the scientific concept of explanation. He is pointing to a complete misunderstanding of that concept that is "the whole modern conception of the world." Wittgenstein has in mind the idea that what was once "explained by reference to God" is now explained by science. In the modern conception the laws of science are taken to replace "the Will of God" as ultimate explanations. But since these laws provide "internal, natural explanations" that appeal to nothing beyond the realm of facts that they explain, "the modern system tries to make it look as if *everything* were explained." Wittgenstein's problem is with the arrogant contention that what the ancient system needed God to do the modern view can do by itself so that everything appears to be explained.

In the sense in which God explained, science explains nothing. And further, the ancients are clearer, for the will of God is a "clear terminus." It is that in terms of which all explanation proceeds, but which is beyond explanation. God's will stands outside what it explains and so sets a clear limit to explanation. The ancient view expresses the limit of all possible explanation by distinguishing between what is to be explained and that in terms of which explanation proceeds. In this way, the utter contingency of everything *in* the world is expressed but only by reference to the noncontingency of something else. And this creates the problem, for the ancient view attempts to ground the contingency of all things in something that can be "spoken about." By so doing it treats God's will as a further item in the world. But this denies the very difference to which the ancient view wants to draw attention. In effect, the ancient view marks a limit only by going beyond that limit. It finds "both sides of the limit thinkable" (*T* preface, p. 3).

In any sense in which science explains, "the Will of God" explains nothing. From the point of view of each, the other explains nothing. The whole aim of the ancient view is to "overcome" the contingency of things by grounding it in the noncontingent but inexplicable. Science cannot achieve any such overcoming because "there is no compulsion making one thing happen because another has happened. The only necessity that exists is *logical* necessity" (*T* 6.37).

The moderns are simply wrong to suppose that they can now do something correctly that the ancients did incorrectly. They are wrong precisely because the sort of explanation science provides cannot avoid the ultimate contingency of all things. "The laws of physics, with all their logical apparatus, still speak, however indirectly, about the objects of the world" (*T* 6.3431). On the other hand, the ancients are clearly wrong to suppose that it is really possible to talk about—say—something that would explain in the sense they demand. "Propositions can express nothing that is higher" (*T* 6.42), and the sort of explanation they want necessarily involves an appeal to the "higher." The ancient view marks the limit of possible explanation but does so in a way that does not attend to the truly radical nature of that limit. The modern view is right to contend against the ancients that their talk of God really does not explain anything. Nothing that could be put into words—said—could provide such an explanation. On the other hand, the ancients are right to see that scientific explanation—an appeal to the laws of nature —cannot provide an explanation that avoids contingency. Scientific "explanations" merely shift the apparent locus of such contingency.

Wittgenstein disagrees with the ancients precisely because they "try to say what cannot be said." But he also disagrees with the modern position because it supposes that having said what can be said—the propositions of natural science—it has done all there is to do. What cannot be achieved by way of science cannot be achieved by metaphysics. But science is not a substitute for metaphysics. The passage quoted earlier from Paul Engelmann again puts the point perfectly when he says of the modern view, it "holds—and this is its essence—that what we can speak about is all that matters in life. *Whereas Wittgenstein passionately believes that all that really matters in human life is precisely what, in his view, we must be silent about*" (*LLW* p. 97). For Wittgenstein, the ancients are right to see that whatever science can say cannot solve their problem. But the moderns are right to see that science is all that can be said. The ancient is wrong to try to say what gives meaning or sense to the world for, after all, it is in that way that God explains. But the ancient is right to insist that the world does have a meaning! As Wittgenstein puts it in the *Notebooks*,

> To believe in God means to see that the facts of the world are not the end of the matter.
> To believe in God means to see that life has a meaning. (*NB* p. 74, 8.7.16)

And, again quoting Engelmann, Wittgenstein "does not doubt that there is such a sense—a doubt which lives at the heart of the modern mood of shiftlessness and insecurity" (*LLW* p. 97). From this we must conclude that Wittgenstein believed in God. What does such a belief involve?

The diagnosis of the joint failure of the ancient and modern world views opens the way to Wittgenstein's own discussion of what is higher precisely by setting aside both science and metaphysics as irrelevant. Science, in the hands of the modernist, denies a meaning to the world, and metaphysics in the guise here of theology tries to build it into the world. It is at this very point that everyone is "just gassing," while Wittgenstein, by rigorously drawing the distinction between what can be said and what can only be "shown," has managed to put everything firmly in place. In order to see this, it is necessary to develop in detail aspects of Wittgenstein's ethical views. This will finally lead back to the connection between the ethical and God via a focus on the ethical subject.

As we have already seen, science exhausts the domain of what can be said. The world is the totality of facts, and language can picture all and only the facts. So if values cannot be located among the facts, they cannot be "put into words." Wittgenstein accepts this point when he says, "It is clear that ethics cannot be put into words. Ethics is transcendental" (T 6.421). But why can't values be located among the facts?

The key point is developed in the "Lecture on Ethics," where Wittgenstein draws a distinction between value terms used in "the trivial or relative sense on the one hand and the ethical or absolute sense on the other" (LE p. 5). The trivial or relative sense covers all uses of value terms in which an object is assessed by reference to a class standard or assigned value relative to a purpose. For example, a good chair is a chair that ranks high among chairs when judged on the basis of the standard criteria for chairs. Or a good hunting dog is a dog that serves the purposes of a hunter well. Standing behind the apparent objectivity of such claims is agreement, explicit or implicit, with regard to the standards of evaluation and/or the purposes to be served by the things evaluated. Value terms used in this way "don't present any difficult or deep problems" (LE p. 5). In fact, judgments that use value terms in this way are merely statements of fact "and can therefore be put in such a form . . . [as to] . . . lose all appearance of a judgment of value" (LE p. 6). For example, for "This is the right road to Nashville" we can substitute "This is the road that will get you to Nashville in the shortest time (or which will serve some other purpose implied or expressed)." Whenever a sentence contains a relative value term, it is possible to find a substitute formulation in which no value term occurs at all and which, nonetheless, expresses the same claim. My purpose here is not to defend this view, but two points should be noted. First, Wittgenstein does not hold that all value terms can be so treated. In fact, he holds that the really interesting ones cannot. Second, various versions of this "reductionist" principle might be formulated depending on the strength of "same claim," but Wittgenstein is not interested in this sort of "philosophical activity."

Relative values are values contingent upon the interest, purposes, or desires of certain individuals or groups—what we might call "empirical wills." This term is meant to refer to the complex of purposes, interests, desires, wants, and so forth that make up the motivational structure of individuals or groups. The term "empirical will" should be understood in the context of our previous terminology concerning the self. The empirical will is a subset of the facts constituting an empirical subject. Such a will is particular, that is to say, it is an item or, more properly, a complex of items in the world. And it is individual—there are, as a matter of fact, a great many such wills. Finally, it is to empirical wills, taken individually or collectively, that relative values are relative. What this means is that fully articulated substitute sentences replacing a relative value claim will always include some motivational facts of the sort that are constitutive of an empirical will. Wittgenstein does not develop this in any detail. In fact, he has no interest in such developments. His attitude here is exactly parallel to that taken with regard to the empirical subject in relation to the problem of solipsism.

The idea that the empirical subject constitutes special philosophical problems has already been shown to derive, at least in part, from confusions surrounding the proper analysis of sentences containing "propositional attitude" verbs. The pseudo-problems surrounding the will as an empirical phenomenon derive from similar sources. Wittgenstein says in the *Notebooks*, "the consideration of willing makes it look as if one part of the world were closer to me than another" (*NB* p. 88, 4.11.16). The will seems to "reach right out" to some events and bring them into being. The connection between the will and *its* actions seems somehow closer and more intimate than with "normal causation." In fact, some philosophers have thought that the will provides us with a direct insight into the causal nexus. But as Wittgenstein adds parenthethically in the passage quoted above, all this is intolerable because it would violate the principle of extensionality so essential to logical atomism.

There are a host of confusions here. The idea that the will gives us a glimpse of the causal nexus betrays misunderstanding not only about willing but also about causation itself. Wittgenstein says, "Belief in the causal nexus is *superstition*" (*T* 5.1361) and goes on to claim, "The freedom of the will consists in the impossibility of knowing actions that still lie in the future. We could know them only if causality were an *inner* necessity like that of logical inference" (*T* 5.1362). Causation is not a form of necessity intermediate between logical necessity and contingency. After all, "There is no compulsion making one thing happen because another has happened. The only necessity that exists is logical necessity" (*T* 6.37). If there is no causal nexus, then the "operations of the will" cannot give direct knowledge of such a nexus. In any case, Wittgenstein asks, "Does not the willed movement of the body happen just like any unwilled movement in the world, but that it is accompanied by the will?" (*NB* p. 88, 4.11.16). Though there are willful actions, there is no special causal history associated with them.

On the other side, the very idea of "acts of will" is misleading, for "the fact that I will an action consists in my performing the action, not in my doing something else which causes the action" (*NB* p. 88, 4.11.16). Here Wittgenstein rejects the idea that there are or need to be distinct acts of will related to specific actions. No doubt, we do what we do willfully, but (and this has a strong *Investigations* tone) that is not a matter of doing two things, one by way of another. Thus even the supposed "act of the will" is a philosophical illusion.

The will does not stand in *any* philosophically interesting or especially intimate relation to "its" acts.

> The world is independent of my will. Even if all that we wish for were to happen still this would only be a favor granted by fate, so to speak: for there is no logical connexion between the will and the world, which would guarantee it. And the supposed physical connexion itself is surely not something that we can will. (*T* 6.373–374)

From the point of view of the will, whether the willed event occurs is "accidental," depending on a vast number of factors that are "surely not something that we could will." This is true because (1) there is no logical connection between will as phenomenon and world, and (2) the supposed physical connection is not within our control, witness the physically disabled (see *NB* p. 76, 21.7.16; p. 86, 20.10.16). By claiming that the world is independent of the will, Wittgenstein is certainly not denying that "in a popular sense there are things that I do, and other things not done by me" (*NB* p. 88, 4.11.16; see also *T* 5.631). This is only to say that there are discoverable regularities with regard to what aspects of human behavior can be brought under self-control.

The relevance of this discussion of the empirical will to our understanding of ethics is exclusively negative. It makes clear that happiness in the "popular sense," that is, the contingent satisfaction of the desires of an empirical will, is without ethical interest. Such happiness, depending as it does on the accidental distribution of events in the world, can at best be of relative value. The will as a phenomenon in the world stands in no special relation to other events. It has no "ethical value," and so no special "theory of the will" is required. Wittgenstein, with characteristic succinctness, sets aside all such issues, saying, "The will as a phenomenon is of interest only to psychology" (*T* 6.432). In the world there exist relative values, and these values are dependent on the empirical will. However, it is just their being in the world and so in the end being *facts* in the world (for the world just is the totality of facts) that makes it impossible for relative values to be ethical values.

The sense of the world must lie outside the world. In the world everything is as it is, and everything happens as it does happen: in it no value exists—and if it did exist, it would have no value.

If there is any value that does have value, it must lie outside of the whole sphere of what happens and is the case. For all that happens and is the case is accidental.

What makes it non-accidental cannot lie *within* the world, since if it did it would itself be accidental. It must lie outside the world. (*T* 6.41)

For there to be values in the world, they must be relative values. But all relative values depend on the accidental character of particular empirical wills, and any value that so depends cannot be an ethical value.

This discussion provides a further insight into the weakness of the ancient world view. We can now see that the theological rendering of the "sense of the world," by treating God's will both as an item in the world insofar as it can be spoken of and as the source of meaning for the world, reduces to nothing more than a cosmic tyranny of one will over all others. God cannot ground ethical value as a metaphysical posit. Even a supremely powerful will, as one will among others, could generate only relative value.

Wittgenstein illustrates the contingent character of relative value by means of the example of a tennis player. When we say to someone who is a bad tennis player that he ought to practice more, we suppose that he or she is interested in playing tennis well. But, as Wittgenstein points out, this may not be true, and if so, our *judgment* is misplaced (LE p. 5). If someone really does not want to play any better, then it simply is not the case that he or she ought to practice more. Whether or not an "ought" applies is therefore contingent on the actual character of a particular will. But that is itself merely one among the totality of facts, and so relative values have no ultimate normative status.

Wittgenstein contrasts the example of the tennis player with someone who, having lied and been told that he has behaved badly, excuses himself by saying that he really does not want to behave any better. The response is totally out of place. The charge that he has behaved badly cannot be deflected by reference to what he wants. Whatever he may want, he *ought* to behave differently. The normative character of such an ethical judgment does not depend on any feature of an empirical will or any other fact. Wittgenstein says, "although all judgments of relative value can be shown to be mere statements of fact, no statement of fact can ever be, or imply, a judgment of absolute value" (LE p. 6). This is precisely what gives such value its special character.

This distinction is surely familiar. In Kantian terminology, it is the distinction between hypothetical and categorical value. Ethics, for Wittgenstein, as that which cannot be put into words, is concerned with categorical value. The merely hypothetical or relative goods are of no philosophical interest, depending directly on an empirical will. Such a will is simply an item in the world but, "It is impossible to speak about the will in so far as it is the subject of ethical attributes" (T 6.423). Again, this is a familiar distinction for us. Our earlier discussion of solipsism revealed two senses of self or subject. One, the metaphysical subject, constitutes the limit of the world and cannot be "put into words." The other, the empirical subject, is an item in the world and can. The ethical will, like the metaphysical subject, must lie beyond the world for if it were merely an item in the world, all value would be relative value and so there would be no ethical value. This is the full import of Wittgenstein's claim that "in the world no value exists—and if it did exist, it would have no value." Ethical value cannot be an item in the world without losing its status as ethical. So, "Ethics is transcendental" (T 6.421). This claim encapsulates two of the most fundamental aspects of Wittgenstein's ethical vision. Ethical value is real, but it is not an item in the world. The world does have a meaning. What can be said, science, is not the end of the matter. It is just in this way that Wittgenstein's

position differs from the positivists'. Any attempt to develop a coherent interpretation of his views must preserve both the reality and
the transcendence of ethical value. Any account that "brings values
into the world" will fail to capture his vision. As we shall see, it is
no simple task to avoid this.

There are a number of passages in the early writings that may
seem to suggest positivism. Consider, for example,

> At the end of my lecture on ethics, I spoke in the first person.
> I believe that it is quite essential. Here nothing more can be
> established. I can only appear as a person speaking for myself.
> (LE p. 16)

and

> And here it is essential that this is not a sociological description
> but that I speak *for myself*. (LE p. 16)

Wittgenstein's point is that if ethics is to be possible, there must
be a "self" that is only a subject and not an object, not an item
capable of "sociological description." However, on a positivist interpretation, "speaking for myself" would mean expressing my own
attitude. "Speaking for oneself" would be a matter of speaking for
a particular individual, for Ludwig Wittgenstein, for example. After
all, the positivists located the essence of ethical language in just this
"expressive" use of terms. So they distinguished between stating the
fact that I approve of a particular state of affairs and actually expressing approval of it. The first is a "sociological description" and
the second, a "value judgment." On this interpretation Wittgenstein
expresses *his* own "personal attitude" at the end of the "Lecture on
Ethics" by speaking for himself. This is why "nothing more can be
established."

Engelmann's insight has already shown that the positivist reading of Wittgenstein's ethical views is wrong. In fact, Wittgenstein disagreed with the whole thrust of positivism just at the point of ethics. As we noted, for Wittgenstein the task of setting the limits of meaningful language was undertaken not for the sake of what falls within those limits but to protect what falls outside. In the "Lecture on Ethics" Wittgenstein clearly indicates that although the attempt to put ethics into words always violates the limits of language, the tendency to do so is something "which I personally cannot help respecting deeply and I would not for my life ridicule it" (LE p. 12). However, Wittgenstein's disagreement with the positivists is not merely about the "value" to be placed on a tendency of the human spirit. Obviously, that disagreement can be given a straightforward positivist reading. Wittgenstein merely expresses a "pro-attitude" to a tendency, to which the positivists express a "con-attitude." Wittgenstein disagrees not simply with the positivists' assessment of a human tendency, he disagrees with the positivist reading of value judgments as such. The problem with it is that it does not preserve their transcendental status. The positivist misconstrues that status as a mere difference in "linguistic roles" and so relocates values "in the world" as expressions of attitude on the part of those who "speak for themselves." In this way, positivism continues the confusion between empirical and transcendental subjectivity. The expressive account of value judgments is, after all, a "reductionism" that Wittgenstein completely rejects.

Wittgenstein is not a positivist in his account of ethics or even of science. As I have argued earlier, transcendental subjectivity—what Wittgenstein calls the "metaphysical subject"—is presupposed by the very "giveness" of the world. The world, even as the mere totality of facts, is *my* world. Transcendental subjectivity is a necessary condition for there being a "*totality* of fact." But this means that since science is "the *totality* of true propositions" (T 4.11), transcendental subjectivity is as much a condition of its possibility as it is of the possibility of ethics. In the *Notebooks* Wittgenstein says, "Only from the consciousness of the *uniqueness of my life* arises religion—science—and art" (*NB* p. 79, 1.8.16). In this passage science is not set over against the more "subjective" (on a positivist reading) matters of religion and art. Rather, each arises in its own way only because "the world is my world." We have already seen how this is true on the logical/metaphysical side of the *Tractatus*, and in the pages that follow we will see what it means both for ethics and religion. (In this connection it is important to remember that "ethics and aesthetics are one and the same" [*T* 6.421]). Wittgenstein is reputed to have said of Carnap that he had no soul. If I am correct, this is not merely a personal comment but a fundamental indictment of his philosophy. Of course, as we have already noted, these two are not unconnected for Wittgenstein.

There is a second interpretation of Wittgenstein's remarks at the end of the lecture that is in keeping with the sense of the *Tractatus* and that takes seriously the claim that "ethics is transcendental." On this view, "speaking for myself" does not mean that one speaks for a specific individual. Rather, it means that if ethical judgments are possible, there must be a subject that is *not* at the same time an object, and the ethical subject is such a subject. Further, if there were no such subject, there would be no "center of the world which we call the I, and which is the bearer of ethics" (*NB* p. 80, 5.8.16). So if there were no I, no "myself," there would be no ethics. In other words, the sense of "myself" at work in these passages is the same sense of "my" in which the "world is *my* world," and that is not one in which the "my" refers to a particular person at all.

What, then, is the nature of the ethical will? The world is the totality of facts, so it can contain nothing of ethical value. "Propositions can express nothing that is higher" (*T* 6.42), but they can express every actual or possible fact. What is of value, then, cannot be an item in the world. Wittgenstein says,

As the subject is not a part of the world but a presupposition of its existence, so good and evil are predicates of the subject, not properties in the world. (*NB* p. 79, 2.8.16)

and

Good and evil only enter through the subject. And the subject is not part of the world, but a boundary of the world. (*NB* p. 79, 2.8.16)

Wittgenstein lays bare his position on the status of the ethical subject in the following passages.

The thinking subject is surely mere illusion. But the willing subject exists.

If the will did not exist, neither would there be that center of the world, which I call the I, and which is the bearer of ethics.

What is good and evil is essentially the I, not the world.

The I, the I is what is deeply mysterious!

The I is not an object. (*NB* p. 80, 5.8.16–7.8.16)

There are, of course, two illusions associated with the thinking subject. One is that individual thinkers and believers are "objects" and as such constitute counterexamples to the thesis of extensionality. We have already shown that this idea is the product of confusion. The second illusion is that associated with metaphysical solipsism in which an individual thinking subject is somehow taken to stand at the limit of the world, constituting a condition for the possibility of the world. But this illusion depends on the confusion of the metaphysical subject and an empirical subject. This "thinking subject" is also an illusion. But the ethical subject—the willing subject—is not the empirical subject. The willing subject exists. "So there really is a way in which there can and must be mention of the I in a *non-psychological sense* in philosophy" (*NB* p. 80, 11.8.16).

There is an interesting difference between the *Tractatus* and the *Notebooks* at this point. In the *Tractatus* it is in connection with the metaphysical subject as the logical limit of all possible representations that Wittgenstein "discovers" that "there really is a sense in which philosophy can talk about the self" (see *T* 5.641). In the *Notebooks*, however, this discovery is made in connection with the willing subject. In fact, in the *Notebooks* the willing subject and the metaphysical subject are much more closely tied together. The subject that is a presupposition of the possibility of the world and representation and the I that is the bearer of ethical properties emerge together. For example, Wittgenstein says, "As my idea is the world, in the same way my will is the world-will" (*NB* p. 85, 15.10.16; see also *NB* p. 79, 2.8.16 and p. 80, 5.8.16). But why, then, is the I mysterious? The metaphysical subject, though a difficult concept, is not mysterious, nor is the empirical subject. The answer lies, I believe, in a deep unclarity in Wittgenstein's own thought. The willing subject, as the condition for the possibility of ethics, must, in the final analysis, be both individual and transcendental. That is, it must, in some sense, be identical with the metaphysical subject and, at the same time, be an individual empirical will. Such a subject is certainly "mysterious." As we unfold Wittgenstein's ethical views, we will begin to see just how far he is able to hold together these apparently incompatible elements. But why is such a hybrid subject necessary for ethics?

To answer this question we must ask another. "What really is the situation of the human will? I will call "will" first and foremost the bearer of good and evil" (*NB* p. 76, 21.7.16). But this willing subject is not an item in the world. It is not an "object" in the technical Tractarian sense—a possible constituent of facts. Rather, the I "objectively confronts every object" (*NB* p. 80, 11.8.16). Ethics is possible only for a transcendental subject. This is merely the logical consequence of the contention that ethics is transcendental, which itself follows from Wittgenstein's notion of absolute value. Thus,

> If the good or bad exercise of the will does alter the world, it can alter only the limits of the world, not the facts—not what can be expressed by means of language.
> In short the effect must be that it becomes an altogether different world. It must, so to speak, wax and wane as a whole.
> The world of the happy man is a different one from that of the unhappy man. (*T* 6.43)

Wittgenstein's views of the happy and unhappy person will be developed later. What we need to see here is that the ethical will stands outside the world, confronting it as a "limited whole." In this respect the ethical and metaphysical subjects are the same. But, there is such a thing as "the good or bad *exercise* of the will." So the ethical subject actually wills the world and wills it in different ways. How can this be true for a transcendental subject? Surely *acts* of will are possible only for individual situated subjects.

The Ethical Subject and Different Worlds

Perhaps we can focus the issues here by asking in what sense the world of the happy person is *a different world* from that of the unhappy person. There only seem to be two alternatives. First, we might suppose that what Wittgenstein means is simply that the happy person takes an attitude to "the totality of facts" different from the unhappy person. This would certainly seem to capture the idea implicit in the previous passage that there are "different exercises of the will"—a happy one and/or an unhappy one. The world as the totality of facts is the one and only world, but the relationship of the ethical subject to that world can differ. The happy person stands in one relationship to the world while the unhappy person stands in another. In each case the world as the totality of facts is unchanged. What is different is the "attitude" of the subject.

But what, then, of the attitude of the happy person? Is it a further item in the world or not? We would certainly seem forced to hold that the world that is the totality of facts *including* the attitude of the happy person and the world that is the totality of facts *including* the attitude of the unhappy person are different, but the difference resides in there being different facts included in each totality, and that is unacceptable. "Ethical transcendence" becomes, at least logically, an item in the world, and this compromises the absoluteness of ethical value because such value becomes a function of the wills of particular individual selves and so relative to them.

If, on the other hand, we suppose that the ethical subject is a transcendental subject in the strictest sense, then the world *is a different world* in the strictest sense. Different subjects would mean different nonoverlapping worlds. There cannot be a world common to more than one transcendental subject. And this means only that the idea of multiple transcendental subjects is nonsense. How, then, can there be a happy person *and/or* an unhappy person? Or if we allow this possibility, how can there be *a world* about which the happy person is happy and the unhappy person, unhappy? If there are different attitudes, these must be had by different subjects or by the same subject at different times. But what does it mean to attribute an attitude, and especially different attitudes, to a transcendental subject? The subject being discussed here must be individual—an item in the world—and this leads us back to the first alternative already discussed. Again, we are in danger of "bringing values into the world" at the cost of robbing them of their ethical value.

If we are forced to accept the first alternative, there is another, and perhaps more problematic, consequence to be noted. If we treat "ethical transcendence" as an attitude that individuals can take to the rest of the world, we are on the verge of admitting various alternative but comprehensive "points of view," and this casts into question the Tractarian notion of "limit." For the limits of a particular perspective are not "the limits of the world." They are simply the limits of a given representation of the world from a point of view. To accept this alternative, then, is to relativize the notion of "limit" in a way that makes the project of the *Tractatus* impossible. We find ourselves confronted with a dilemma analogous to that which we discovered concerning the metaphysical subject itself. On the first alternative we preserve the "unity of the world" only by abandoning the transcendence of the ethical subject and with it the ethical status of value. At the same time that we abandon the transcendence of the ethical subject, we also relativize the notion of "limit" essential to the whole project of the *Tractatus*. On the other hand and on the second alternative, even if we can preserve the transcendence of the ethical subject, we must abandon the unity of the world. In the context of the *Tractatus* this means solipsism.

Perhaps the problem can be solved simply by drawing a distinction between different levels. There can be two different sorts of answers—one formal and the other concrete—to the question, "Who is happy or unhappy?" Formally, the answer is the ethical subject as the subject for which *the world has become my world* (what this actually means in ethical terms is the subject of the next chapter). Concretely, the answer might be Michael Hodges or Ludwig Wittgenstein, in virtue of a certain attitude which each of them takes to the rest of the world. The previous discussion simply ignores the legitimate difference between these two levels. When Wittgenstein talks about "the happy man," he is talking about a certain possibility of willing—what might be called "willing the world at the limit"—not about any particular acts of will. Further, to will the world at the limit is to will it in such a way that the will is fulfilled—is happy—independently of *any and every* particular feature of the world so that it is not a mere matter of fact that the happy person is happy although it is a mere matter of fact that Michael Hodges is.

Although this distinction may offer a plausible way to understand aspects of Wittgenstein's view, it is not adequate. In the first place, it offers no account of the difference between the happy and unhappy person. I do not mean that it does not specify what that difference is. That will be the task of the next chapter. What I mean here is that it does not explain how there could be such a difference. The problem is still, how it is possible to will the world "at the limit" but to will it differently? For the metaphysical subject, to grasp the totality of facts just is to "see" the world from the logical limit. At this point there is no room for alternatives, and yet, for the ethical will, it is essential that there is such a possibility.

What, then, is the relation between the metaphysical subject and the ethical subject? In one highly provocative passage Wittgenstein considers the question directly.

> But can we conceive a being that isn't capable of Will at all, but only of Idea (seeing for example)? In some sense this seems impossible. But if it were possible then there could also be a world without ethics. (*NB* p. 77, 21.7.16)

The intuition seems to be that for a mere observer the world is only the totality of *facts*—everything is as it is. There is no room for value. As Wittgenstein puts it, for a merely observing metaphysical subject—one for which there is only "seeing" for example—"all propositions are of equal value" (*T* 6.4), which is to say, of no value at all.

But how does willing bring value to the world? Two interpretations seem possible here. On the first, which is Kantian in spirit, we might contend that even though there would be value—good and bad—nothing would have specifically ethical value without will. On this view, we would distinguish between something good or bad happening and that happening's having ethical value. If a tree falls and kills someone, that is a bad thing, but there is no ethical evil involved. In order for the killing to be ethically bad, it must have been willed. What is ethically evil, on this view, is willing the death, not the event itself. So without the ethical will there would be a world without ethics.

Now, there are very clear Kantian aspects to Wittgenstein's ethical vision. Some have already been identified, and others will be developed in greater detail in the next chapter. There is even a sense in which it is true that it is only what is willed that is good and evil. "[T]he world in itself is neither good nor evil" (*NB* p. 79, 2.8.16). Rather, "good and evil only enter through the *subject*" (*NB* p. 79, 2.8.16). And, of course, the subject here is the willing subject. However, there is one aspect of this account that finally will not do for Wittgenstein, and that is its focus on particular action. No particular action, willed or otherwise, can have ethical value just because it is an item in the world. For the will as ethical subject there is an internal connection between the will and what it wills since the world of the happy person is a different world from the world of the unhappy person. Therefore, ethics cannot be a matter of anything done in the world. Only the limits of the world are altered. Now, the point is that on the Kantian interpretation what is willed is an action, that is, some event in the world. It may be irrelevant to the moral worth of the will that the event occurs or not, but nonetheless what is willed is a particular action. So on this interpretation the will as the condition of the possibility of ethics would be aiming at bringing about some change in the world. And this is simply inconsistent with what Wittgenstein says. As we shall see in the next chapter, the ethical will in its ultimate fulfillment aims at bringing about nothing, for what is, is what ought to be. It is rather for the will to come to "own" and "appreciate" what is as what ought to be.

There is a second way in which the will may be seen to bring value to the world. Suppose that the will is treated as a principle of interest. (I am tempted to call this an "Aristotelian" interpretation.) To have a will, in this view, is to have interests, that is to say, desires, projects, hopes, concerns, and the like. Now, once interests are introduced into the world, some objects become important. They come to have value, acquiring "meaning" in relation to the various projects of an interested subject.

This alternative may appear plausible only as an account of how relative value comes *into* the world since by making reference to the "various projects of interested subjects," the will is taken to be a particular will, and so the value that it "brings into the world" must be relative value. But, just as the subject for which the world is the totality of facts is not a particular subject but the possibility of representation, so the will for which the world is ethically good or bad is simply the possibility of willing. Thus the world is *the* ethical world in virtue of the *possibility* of willing, just as the world is the *totality* of facts in virtue of the *possibility* of representation. The ethical subject wills the world from the limit just as the metaphysical subject "sees" the world from the limit. In each case all the specific details of the actual world are irrelevant. The metaphysical subject does not determine any particulars of the world, nor does the ethical subject. "This is connected with the fact that no part of our experience is at the same time *a priori*. Whatever we see could be other than it is. Whatever we can describe at all could be other than it is" (*T* 5.634). It is from the point of view of the metaphysical subject that the limits of all possible representation are set, so, of course, it must leave open every possibility. Similarly, it is from the point of view of the ethical subject—the willing subject—that the limits of willing are set, so it must leave open every possibility. The ethical subject wills *the world*. It does not will this or that fact in the world. What this means we will have occasion to see in the next chapter.

So, if we could conceive a being without will, but only idea, we could conceive a being for which the world is nothing more than the totality of facts. For such a being there would be no value, and we would, therefore, have conceived a "world without ethics."

The terminology of "will" and "idea," so obviously borrowed from Schopenhauer, sets the issue. Could there be a metaphysical subject that was not, at the same time, the ethical subject? If there could, then "there could also be a world without ethics." But the possibility is apparently only entertained to be rejected, for Wittgenstein goes on to say, "Ethics must be a condition of the world, like logic" (NB p. 77, 24.7.16). So the willing subject must be a condition of the world just as the metaphysical subject is.

Is the ethical subject the condition of the world as the totality of facts or as the world of the happy or unhappy person? These must be two quite distinct senses of "world," for it makes no sense to suppose that there is more than one "totality of facts" while it must be the case that the world of the happy person is a different world from that of the unhappy person. Wittgenstein seems to recognize this when he says, "If I am right, then it is not sufficient for the ethical judgment that a world be given" (NB p. 79, 2.8.16). The mere givenness of the world (there being a visual field, as it were) is not yet sufficient to ethics, even though the metaphysical subject is already implicated in that givenness. The world as given, as open to representation, yields the notion of the metaphysical subject, but on Wittgenstein's account here, it does not yield the ethical subject. The metaphysical subject does not constitute the condition of the possibility of the "world" of the happy person, for the metaphysical subject, as the possibility of representation, does not "will" the world. However, if there is no willing subject, there would be no center to the world—no I—that is the bearer of ethics. The ethical subject cannot be the metaphysical subject as such. But then, what is their relation?

Wittgenstein's problems run very deep here. If "the world of the happy man is a different one from that of the unhappy man," then there must be some difference between that ethical subject for which there is a happy world and that for which there is an unhappy one. The difference cannot be "in the world," for "the good or bad exercise of the will can alter only the limits of the world not the facts" (T 6.43). But how are we to understand this difference with regard to the ethical subject? At a minimum, there are either two distinct subjects or two distinct moments in a single subject. It will not do at this point to say that the world is subjectively different while it is objectively the same, precisely because the possibility of drawing that distinction depends on contrasting how the world appears for one subject as opposed to another and so compromises the very unity it is meant to defend. For the transcendental subject, the subjective/objective distinction makes no sense.

At the heart of Wittgenstein's treatment of solipsism is the claim that the "self of solipsism shrinks to a point without extension, and there remains the reality co-ordinate with it" (T 5.64). The metaphysical subject is in no sense an individual subject. It is merely the possibility of representation. That is, it is language taken as the possibility of representation. What is critical for the "refutation of solipsism" is that the metaphysical subject "disappear"—the medium of representation must become invisible so that what it represents is all that remains. If the logical unity of the metaphysical subject is in any way compromised, solipsism reemerges. But it is that unity which is sacrificed by Wittgenstein's account of the ethical will, for it requires us to conceive the notion of an individual transcendental subject. The full meaning of this claim will become clearer when we have developed Wittgenstein's account of happiness in the next chapter.

Perhaps the most the argument has shown to this point is that the concept of the metaphysical subject is different from that of the ethical subject. But it does not follow that the metaphysical subject is not the ethical subject. Even though we "come to" the ideas differently, it does not follow that they are necessarily ideas of different things. To take a classic example, "the morning star" is a distinct concept from that of "the evening star," but the morning star is the evening star.

This response will not do for two reasons. First, the ethical subject must be particular and situated in just the way that the metaphysical subject cannot be. That is, it is not simply that the two notions involve different properties, they necessarily involve incompatible properties. But second, the intuition behind the reply is totally unacceptable. That intuition is that the metaphysical subject is a "thing" that can be referred to by different descriptions, some of which are only contingently true of it. But surely this is exactly the view of the metaphysical subject that Wittgenstein wants to expose as absurd. The metaphysical subject is not a thing that the arguments in the *Tractatus* lead us to "discover," but that we might have run across in another independent way. This is why the morning star/evening star case is a badly misleading analogy. In fact, if we were to accept that analogy, Wittgenstein's treatment of solipsism would fall apart of its own weight. If the metaphysical subject is a thing in this sense, then the claim that the world is my world takes on a meaning in which the subject does not "shrink to a point."

Wittgenstein's account of ethics requires a subject that is at the same time transcendental and individual. If, as seems clearly implied by the ethical views, there must be more than one ethical subject, then the world is only the world for a particular subject. But this means that the claim that the world is *my* world takes on a devastating meaning. Wittgenstein's treatment of solipsism depends essentially on a radical and clear distinction between the empirical subject and the metaphysical subject. It now appears that Wittgenstein's treatment of ethics essentially involves a confusion of these two notions. The ethical subject is and must be transcendental, but at the same time it must be individual and situated, that is, a particular will among other wills. Only then could it make sense to talk of happy *and/or* unhappy wills. Thus, if we take seriously Wittgenstein's treatment of solipsism, we cannot accept his account of ethics, and vice versa. If the transcendental subject is a particular situated subject, there is no way to avoid metaphysical solipsism within the structure of the *Tractatus*. And if we accept the "refutation of solipsism," there is no way to give an account of ethics.

Before leaving this discussion, focus once more on the contention that there cannot be idea without will. If there cannot be a "world without ethics," as early Wittgenstein holds, then we cannot have observation without will. What this means in the context of the *Tractatus* is that as there is pure observation that has for its object the totality of facts, so there must also be a pure willing that has for its object that same totality. Both observing and willing are understood transcendentally for the project of the *Tractatus*.

Seen in the context of the *Philosophical Investigations*, however, that same claim—that there can be no observation without will—takes on a radically different and even "destructive" meaning for the project of the *Tractatus*. What it means is that all observation is interested. There is no "pure observation" and so no such thing as "*the* totality of facts" as its objective correlate. What we call "objective observing" is itself a particular situated and interested way of describing the rest of the world that is no doubt different in important ways from other "language games" but that cannot determine "*the* totality of facts." Rather, there are various "totalities," various language games, identified and understood against a background of interests shared by a community of language users—what the later Wittgenstein calls a form of life.

Seen from the Tractarian perspective, such claims can be nothing more than irrelevant empirical observations. Of course, there are many languages, but, after all, they are all languages, and it is the task of the *Tractatus* to specify the limits of all possible languages qua language. For that task the differences are irrelevant—what we seek to articulate is the "general form of a proposition." Or if the multiplicity is itself understood transcendentally, a new form of solipsism emerges. For the *Tractatus* a language presupposes a subject, so a real multiplicity of languages would involve a multiplicity of subjects, each with "its own language," the limits of which would be the limits of *its* world. But if this multiplicity is taken without the priority of unity implicit in the transcendental project, one is led to a position that involves a rejection of the very ideas of "totality" and "limit" that are so fundamental to the project of the *Tractatus*. The only limits there are, are the limits of particular language games, and these are always "seen" from the point of view of some other interested project as well as being open to modification and revision. On this view it can make no sense to even propose the sort of project that defines the *Tractatus*. The claim that will and idea are essentially interconnected makes impossible the very transcendence that that project presupposes.

If our discussion of ethics in the *Tractatus* is correct up to this point, one can begin to see how the difficulties that surround the notion of the ethical subject might serve as a transition point to the later philosophy. The ethical subject is at one and the same time situated, particular, and transcendental. The only way to accommodate this sort of notion is to relativize "transcendence" so that it simply means being in some sense beyond a particular domain where that "being beyond" is itself situated in another field. Wittgenstein seems to be struggling toward this notion of "situated transcendence," but the "language of the *Tractatus*" is incapable of articulating it. Once "language" is no longer treated as a single unity, once real diversity becomes acceptable, the notion of transcendence can be displaced by "situated difference."

More will be said about this in the final chapter, but I hope the reader can begin to see how continued reflection on the "problem of subjectivity" in the *Tractatus* stands at the center of the move from the *Tractatus* to the *Philosophical Investigations*.

6

ETHICS AND HAPPINESS

Three Suppositions

There are three distinct claims that form the background for Wittgenstein's account of the relation of ethical goodness and happiness. First, there is his view that the will is impotent. He says, "The world is independent of my will" (*T* 6.373), and in the *Notebooks* he says, "I cannot bend the world to my will. I am completely powerless" (*NB* p. 73, 11.6.16). Although we have already developed some aspects of his view of the will, a closer look will be necessary.

Second, there is a Stoic, Kantian thesis that ethics must deal with what pertains to the will as such.

> When an ethical law of the form, 'Thou shalt . . .', is laid down, one's first thought is, 'And what if I do not do it?' It is clear, however, that ethics has nothing to do with punishment and reward in the usual sense of the terms. So our question about the consequences of an action must be unimportant.—At least those consequences should not be events. For there must be something right about the question we have posed. There must indeed be some kind of ethical reward and ethical punishment, but they must reside in the action itself.
>
> (And it is also clear that the reward must be something pleasant and the punishment something unpleasant.) (*T* 6.422)

Now, given the first thesis—that the will is impotent—no "events" can be relevant to the assessment of the will since they all stand outside its power. But this means that as ethical subject, the will cannot be judged on the basis of what it accomplishes. In fact, "If the good or bad exercise of the will does alter the world, it can alter only the limits of the world, not the facts (T 6.43). So reward and punishment, in order to be ethically relevant, must be implicit in the "action" of the ethical subject itself. Mere consequences will not do. Nor can reward and punishment be "imposed" from without, say, by God's will, since this would reduce all value to relative value. Reward and punishment in the traditional sense will be ethically irrelevant. What is relevant must pertain to the ethical subject as such, and we have seen that that subject is a will. What pertains to a will as such is simply what it wills.

A third and apparently incompatible thesis is also implicit in the previous passage. There must indeed be some kind of ethical reward and punishment, and that must be something pleasant or unpleasant. Set alongside the Stoic/Kantian theme is a deep Aristotelian sense that ethics must be a matter of happiness and unhappiness. At one point Wittgenstein says simply,

> I am either happy or unhappy, that is all. It can be said: Good and evil do not exist. (NB p. 74, 8.7.16)

and

> I keep on coming back to this! simply the happy life is good, the unhappy bad. And if I now ask myself: But why should I live *happily*, then this of itself seems to me to be a tautological question; the happy life seems to be justified, of itself, it seems that it is the only right life. (NB p. 78, 30.7.16)

Wittgenstein may be holding either that to be good and to be happy are the same or that one logically involves the other or that in the end there is no goodness, only happiness. For our purposes the differences between these are irrelevant, and I will treat them as a single view, namely, the view that goodness is intimately related to happiness. What Wittgenstein cannot be holding is the view that *as a matter of fact* goodness brings happiness as a consequence. That is completely antithetical to the Kantian theme that we have identified, and it reduces ethical value to relative value. This last position is irrelevant.

But happiness in the usual sense clearly does depend on a variety of accidental features that are beyond the power of the will, and this creates a tension in the triad of theses we are discussing. If what is beyond the will's power cannot be relevant to its ethical assessment, how can goodness and happiness be intimately related? Either Wittgenstein must offer an account of happiness and the powers of the will in which happiness is within its powers, or he must reject the Stoic, Kantian thesis. If ethical goodness is intimately tied to happiness and if an ethical assessment must be based on what is within the power of the will as such, then happiness must be within the power of the will, in which case the will is not powerless. We must examine more carefully the doctrine of the impotence of the will along with Wittgenstein's account of happiness.

The will as an empirical phenomenon is powerless. However, this does not mean that, as things stand, there is no regular "connection" between "acts of the will" and certain bodily events. Normally, our bodies do what we want them to within clear limits. It is Wittgenstein's contention, however, that such a regular connection is, strictly taken, a "gift of fate." All the "powers of the will" are accidental. They can be stripped away since there is no logical connection between willing and fulfillment. This "powerlessness" is simply an immediate consequence of the atomism of the *Tractatus*. Insofar as an act's being willed and its occurring are distinct facts, it is possible for each to obtain while the other does not. That is what Wittgenstein means when he says, "it is a fact of logic that wanting does not stand in any logical connexion with its fulfilment" (*NB* p. 77,

29.7.16). There can be no logical relation that grounds an inference from one distinct event to another, and "belief in the causal nexus is *superstition*."

The impotence of the individual empirical will derives directly from its being in the world. However, the ethical subject, as we have seen, is not in the midst of things but confronts the world as its equivalent, and its impotence derives from that (*NB* p. 86, 4.11.16). Since it is absolutely beyond the world, it cannot intervene in the "totality of facts." Again, as Wittgenstein says, "If the good or bad exercise of the will does alter the world, it can alter only the limits of the world, not the facts" (*T* 6.43). The ethical subject confronts the world as an already given totality, so change within that totality is out of the question. In this sense the will does not act in the world but "is an attitude of the subject to the world" (*NB* p. 87, 4.11.16).

So there is a sense in which the ethical will is completely impotent since it accomplishes nothing *in the world*. But it is also utterly potent. There is an internal connection between will and fulfillment. The effect of the exercise of the ethical will "must be that the world becomes an altogether different world" (*T* 6.43) so that "[t]he world of the happy is *a happy world*" (*NB* p. 78, 29.7.16). The ethical subject can by its acts transform the world not in detail but into an altogether different world. This transformation does not alter the facts; it alters the meaning, value, or significance of the facts. That is something that "happens" from without. Wittgenstein drives this to its logical conclusion when he says, "Going by the above, then, the willing subject would have to be happy or unhappy, and happiness or unhappiness could not be part of the world" (*NB* p. 79, 2.8.16). Happiness or unhappiness is a feature of the willing subject, and the willing subject is not part of the world, so happiness and unhappiness are not. It appears that we need to distinguish between empirical happiness—the satisfaction of our desires in the world— and transcendental or ethical happiness. Empirical happiness would consist in the regular and systematic satisfaction of one's particular desires, whatever they happen to be. Obviously, this depends on what Wittgenstein refers to as a "gift of fate" and what we would certainly call good fortune. It is the sort of happiness possessed in the best circumstances (at least in novels) by the unreflective middle class. In any case, it is ethically without value, precisely because it depends on what is, strictly speaking, beyond the will. Its value can only be relative. Transcendental or ethical happiness, on the other hand, must be a feature of the ethical subject itself. It is, as Wittgenstein says, a matter of the will's being in "agreement with the world" (*NB* p. 75, 8.7.16).

What, then, is the nature of the transformation that is the "effect" of the willing ethical subject? At the most general level, at least, the answer can already be stated. Since Wittgenstein has said that the will is an attitude of the subject to the world, he is in a position to suggest that the attitude that one takes to the world transforms it into a different world. Of course, this transformation does not change any of the facts. Rather, it changes the meaning or significance of the facts. Further, it must be Wittgenstein's view that this attitude of the subject is sufficient to happiness. In this way he can satisfy all three of the theses that we discussed. Ethics is a matter of what the will wills as such. What the will wills is not an act in the world but an attitude to the world. And finally, that attitude is sufficient to happiness. In broad outline, this is Wittgenstein's view. But what specifically is this attitude of the happy person?

Three Modes of the Ethical

In the *Notebooks* and elsewhere, Wittgenstein presents three distinct but related accounts of happiness to be called here the stoic, the moral, and the aesthetic. It is by no means clear what the relationship between these alternatives is in Wittgenstein's own thought. Although he does not always seem fully aware of the differences between them, at times he is acutely aware of the difficulties facing one or the other. Perhaps he moves through the stoic and the moral levels and finally accepts the aesthetic. There is some evidence to support such a view. For example, given that the *Notebooks* is not a single finished work but one that presents ideas in development, and that the aesthetic is discussed near the end, it might be reasonable to conclude that that view was Wittgenstein's final position. This reading has the advantage of focusing attention on what is clearly the most fully consistent position that Wittgenstein offers. On the other hand, perhaps the stoic and moral are never rejected but are treated as levels in an assent leading to the final aesthetic stage. Certainly the stoic can be seen as complementary to and preparatory for the aesthetic. However, the moral level does not so easily fit into such a structure.

What I propose here is to examine in some detail the moral stage, making it possible to develop a systematic critique of it, which may have been anticipated by Wittgenstein himself (see *NB* pp. 77–78, 29.7.16, and my discussion below). That critique will motivate a turn to the stoic stage as preparatory to, and an element in, the aesthetic.

Although this way of structuring the discussion is not meant as a definitive interpretation, it does provide a constructive and coherent way of presenting the many strands of Wittgenstein's ethical thought, and it focuses attention on the aesthetic, which, I will argue, is the only view that can plausibly be sustained within the logical structure of the *Tractatus*. There is a final point to make about the terminology: throughout I use the term "moral" to name the specific stage, mode, or level to be discussed below and reserve the term "ethical" for Wittgenstein's treatment of value as absolute.

The Moral

Perhaps more distinctly than any other aspect of his personality, Wittgenstein's strong moral sense pervades his personal life. It is also characteristic of him to direct his judgment toward himself, not to the world. Engelmann comments on this when he says,

In me Wittgenstein unexpectedly met a person who . . . suffered acutely under the discrepancy between the world as it is and as it ought to be according to his lights, but who tended *also* to seek the source of that discrepancy within, rather than without, himself. This was an attitude which . . . was vital for any true understanding or meaningful discussion of his own spiritual condition. (*LLW* pp. 74–75, my emphasis)

When Engelmann says here that he "tended *also* to seek the source of the discrepancy within," I take him to be saying that both he and Wittgenstein sought such a source. It is "vital for any true understanding" not only of Wittgenstein's spiritual condition but also of his philosophical remarks on value, particularly the example of guilt discussed in the "Lecture on Ethics" and the notion of conscience presented in the *Notebooks*.

In the lecture Wittgenstein offers three examples of experiences that are supposed to give some content to the notion of absolute or ethical value. The first two are the experiences of "wonder at the existence of the world" and "absolute safety." Of course, these descriptions are both, strictly speaking, nonsensical. Although it makes perfect sense to wonder at *how* things are—that they are this way as opposed to that way since things might be otherwise—for Wittgenstein, it makes no sense to wonder at the very existence of the world. The metaphysical proposition "Nothing exists" is, given Wittgenstein's picture theory of language, a pseudo-proposition. If it were true, it would picture nothing (since there would be nothing to picture) and so would be meaningless. Or to put the point the other way around, if it is true, then it pictures a certain fact that given its truth exists, in which case it is false. But if it is a pseudo-proposition, then neither it nor its negation—something exists—express a fact, and so nothing requires explanation.

Now, if it makes no sense to wonder at the existence of the world, it also makes no sense to suppose that we are absolutely safe. We can be safe from this or that danger or from all "normal" or "usual" dangers but not "absolutely safe." Only if one could escape all the contingencies of the world would such a state of security be possible. So here again we are drawn out of the world to a transcendent perspective from which the totality of facts appears as a limited whole. From there the world's very existence is a wonder that calls for explanation. From there we are safe from all possibilities—absolutely safe. These experiences almost demand a theological articulation. After all, it is only in the "hand of God" that we can be absolutely safe (LE p. 10). It is the transcendence implicit in these descriptions that refers us to the ethical dimension.

The last example, that of guilt, is no exception, for it is not guilt with regard to this act or that happening, but "guilt before God" (LE p. 10). And this is guilt in relation to the whole world since

How things stand [the world], is God.
God is, how things stand [the world]. (NB p. 79, 1.8.16)

As with the other two, this experience cannot be put into words since in the world it is "undeniable that . . . there are things that I do, and other things not done by me" (NB p. 88, 4.11.16). Guilt before the world would only be appropriate for God—the being responsible for the whole world. Remember, however, that for Wittgenstein ethically "the world is given to me, i.e. my will enters into the world completely from outside" (NB p. 74, 8.7.16). As ethical subject the world is co-relative to my will, and so there can be total responsibility and therefore guilt in relation to it. As with each of the other examples, Wittgenstein's notion of guilt locates the subject outside what it experiences—as a subject that "transcends" the world. But how is guilt possible for such a subject?

Perhaps an example will help to clarify the issue. Consider the Holocaust. Since the will is powerless, any action may have no effect, and even if it were to, that would only be as a "favor granted by fate." Now, someone who, knowing about the Holocaust, still does nothing might reason as follows. "I am not responsible for these events. I do not do them; I cannot prevent them. I can only accept them." A "proper view of the world" would seem to make guilt impossible, leaving one free to ignore the events of the world. But surely that cannot be the case. Nothing that gets done *or* is left undone can have any value.

What is misconceived here is the self/world dichotomy. It is only from within the world that there are acts that one does or does not do. Only an empirical will could reason as above, excusing itself from guilt in relation to a particular set of actions that are, *as a matter of fact,* beyond its control. Of course, an empirical will is not responsible for the whole world; it is merely an item in that world. But an empirical will is not the ethical subject. It is not me as this particular individual that is morally responsible or guilty in any case. The relevant dichotomy for ethics is the dichotomy between the self and the world, including myself as a particular will.

Consider a second individual who, knowing of the Holocaust and recognizing that all his or her efforts may fail—the will is powerless—nonetheless bends every effort to stop it. For our first individual the totality of facts that is confronted "objectively" is the world in which the Holocaust occurs *and* in which the individual makes no attempt to do anything. But that is a world in which the will is *not* set against the Holocaust. It is acceptable that there be the Holocaust *and* that he or she do nothing. It is this totality of facts—this world—that the ethical subject must evaluate. The state of one's will is itself an item in the world that one must be in "agreement with." In the second case the world is again one in which the Holocaust occurs but it is also one in which the will of the individual is set against it. It is not important that anything actually happen in this second case, for we could

imagine a man who could use none of his limbs and hence could in the ordinary sense, not exercise his *will.* He could, however, think and *want* and communicate his thoughts to someone else. Could therefore do good or evil through the other man. Then it is clear that ethics would have validity for him, too, and that he in the *ethical sense* is the bearer of a *will*. (*NB* pp. 76–77, 21.7.16)

Wittgenstein's own thought is clearly in transition here for he is still holding on to the idea that there must be some access to action *in* the world if only "through the other man." But in the final analysis this continues the misconception identified above. It makes no difference what actually gets done in the world. What does make a difference is that there is a will that accepts or is set against the Holocaust. Efforts are, at best, merely signs of the sincerity of the will's opposition or agreement.

The world is the totality of facts including facts about myself as a will. If I do not find myself acceptable, if my assessment of myself always finds myself lacking, then I will be fundamentally unhappy. I am responsible for the world that contains both the Holocaust and my own attitude toward it. But since this is true for everything in the world, my responsibility and, if I find myself unacceptable, "my guilt" are pervasive.

Here we have in clear outline a conceptual development of the suggestion taken from Engelmann's earlier comments. Both he and Wittgenstein turn inward, for the fault is not to be found in the world. The "discrepancy" between life as it is and as it ought to be is "not the fault of life as it is, but of myself as I am" (*LLW* p. 77). Engelmann goes on to say that Wittgenstein "saw life as a task."

Moreover, he looked upon all the features of life as it is, that is to say upon all facts, as an essential part of the conditions of that task; just as a person presented with a mathematical problem must not try to ease his task by modifying the problem. (*LLW* p. 79)

In the final analysis, action to "modify the problem" is impossible and irrelevant. The ethical will is impotent! The task is simply to live consistently with oneself. As Wittgenstein says, "In order to live happily *I* must be in agreement with the world. And that is what 'being happy' means" (*NB* p. 75, 8.7.16). And conversely, if I cannot be in agreement with the world, if in my view there is a discrepancy between the world as it is and as it ought to be, the fault is with me. I am guilty before the world!

Now, this moral assessment of myself cannot merely be another judgment of an empirical will. As such it would be perspectival and relative and so would lack the character of an ethical judgment. As Wittgenstein says, "in it [the world] no value exists—and if it did exist, it would have no value" (*T* 6.41). To be truly ethical the judgment must come from beyond the totality of fact that it judges, but that totality contains all the facts including my attitude to those facts.

The author of an autobiography provides a model for understanding the point here, for when he or she passes judgment on a past life of crime and depravity, the author must be beyond that life so as to judge it. Otherwise, the assessment is merely that of a depraved criminal and deserves no attention. The very logic of this autobiographical assessment requires two "selves," and it requires that the self that makes the judgment be "stationed beyond" the one that it judges. If we come to suspect that the judgment of depraved criminality is itself made by that very depraved criminal, we will have a right to wonder for what depraved purposes the judgment is being presented.

This necessity for two levels underlies Wittgenstein's comments on conscience. He asks,

How can man be happy at all, since he cannot ward off the misery of this world?

Through the life of knowledge.

> The good conscience is the happiness that the life of knowledge preserves.

> The life of knowledge is the life that is happy in spite of the misery of the world. (*NB* p. 81, 13.8.16)

What is the good conscience and what is the life of knowledge? Let us begin with the good conscience. That idea, even in its ordinary employment, is certainly connected with the possibility of self-evaluation and guilt. It is my conscience that tries to dissuade me from doing those awful things and then refuses to relent when I have done them.

The notion of conscience, for Wittgenstein, is connected with the expanded sense of "world" developed earlier. The point is alluded to when Wittgenstein says:

> When my conscience upsets my equilibrium, then I am not in agreement with Something. But what is this? Is it *the world*?
> Certainly it is correct to say: Conscience is the voice of God. (*NB* p. 75, 8.7.16)

Remember that for Wittgenstein "there are two godheads: The world and my independent I" (*NB* p. 74, 8.7.16). Conscience, as the voice of God, is the ethical subject as it assesses the totality of facts that includes myself as a particular will. Such judgments of conscience become acutely apparent when a will is divided against itself. "For example: it makes me unhappy to think that I have offended such and such a man. Is that my conscience?" (*NB* p. 75, 8.7.16). Again we discover two "selves." One is the self that offends such and such a man, and the other is the self that cannot accept the offense and is made unhappy. But if this unhappiness is to be ethically relevant, the self that "has" it must be beyond the world. In this way the "good conscience" is a will that is in agreement with itself and, by so being, with the world.

We can now see what Wittgenstein means by the "life of knowledge." It is a life based, not on detailed information about the course of events, that is, scientific information, but on a view of the world taken as a whole. Knowledge, in the first sense, would be of interest only to a particular situated will trying to anticipate and control the course of events. The life of knowledge is a life founded on the knowledge *shown* in the *Tractatus*, for example, that the world is the totality of facts, that the will is powerless, or that ethics concerns the limits of the world, not the facts, and so on. Having abandoned the hope of control within the order of things, we are left with autobiographical transcendence and the project of maintaining the integrity of the will, that is, a good conscience.

As we saw in our discussion of the Holocaust, it would be a mistake to suppose that this view leads to nonaction as a particular way of being *in* the world. Nonaction in the world is no more implied than is action of any kind. Autobiographical transcendence does not depend on rejecting anything in particular about the world, and so in one sense everything may go on as before. What is changed is not any particular fact in the world but rather the "limits" of the world. What is changed is the meaning of the totality of facts, not the totality itself.

The notion of transcendence employed here can now be brought more clearly into focus. For autobiographical transcendence the will as object of judgment is distinct from the will as judge, and it is the will as judge that has ethical status. But is this form of transcendence sufficient for Wittgenstein's notion of value? It certainly does not follow from the fact that the author of an autobiography, in evaluating his or her life, must station himself or herself beyond the particular projects that constitute the fabric of that life, that such an author is not an item in the world in the logical sense. The author of an autobiography is, after all, a particular individual who passes judgment, say, on his or her criminal past from a particular point of view. But then autobiographical transcendence is only a limited "psychological" transcendence, not the logical transcendence of the metaphysical subject. However, nothing short of the latter will support the claims that Wittgenstein makes about value.

The situated character of autobiographical transcendence can be brought clearly into focus if we reconsider the problem of guilt. As we saw, autobiographical transcendence is presupposed by the guilt Wittgenstein discusses in the "Lecture on Ethics." However, that guilt is possible for autobiographical transcendence also shows that it is not absolute transcendence. A clear distinction must be maintained between responsibility for the world as the totality of facts and guilt in the face of that totality. The former is clearly the necessary consequence of the transcendence of the ethical subject. To confront the world as a given totality—to will it as a totality—is to be responsible for that totality, but guilt is a particular "coloration" of responsibility. In Engelmann's terms, it is to suffer "acutely under the discrepancy between the world as it is and as it ought to be" *and* to find the source of the discrepancy within oneself. A will that absolutely transcended the world would be indifferent to every particular fact *in the world,* even including facts about its own attitudes to the world. But in that case guilt is impossible. The very possibility of guilt, which requires transcendence, also discloses its "limited" character. It is just the possibility of dual attitudes that exposes the situated character of the will here. That the self of autobiographical transcendence can be guilty *or* achieve the life of good conscience firmly locates that self within the world as one item among others.

Wittgenstein seems to have recognized this in a comment about himself in one of his letters to Paul Engelmann. He writes,

> I am in a state of mind that is terrible to me. I have been through it several times before; it is the state of *not being able to get over a particular fact.* It is a pitiable state, I know. But there is only one remedy that I can see, and that is of course to come to terms with that fact. (*LLW* p. 33)

It makes no difference what "particular fact" Wittgenstein has in mind. Speculation about his personal life at this point is philosophically irrelevant and even odious. In fact, such speculation, insofar as it is taken seriously, betrays a total misunderstanding of the point. It is the fact of guilt that is relevant, not what that guilt might be about. That one cannot "get over a particular fact" shows a failure on the part of the person to transcend the particularity of one's situation even if that concerns not facts about the world "in the popular sense," but facts about one's self.

Thus the self of autobiographical transcendence is still a particular will that "transcends" the world in a limited and psychological, though perhaps interesting, way. While autobiographical transcendence may offer a viable method for achieving a certain contentment *in the world,* it is a strategy of a particular will that is still an item within the totality of facts. As such, it does not offer a basis for understanding Wittgenstein's radical contentions about value.

Wittgenstein may have recognized this problem. At least, he seems to have been aware of the difficulties in developing an adequate theory of the will. He says,

> Is it possible to will good, to will evil and not to will?
>
> Or is only he happy who does *not* will?
>
> "To love one's neighbour" means to will!
>
> But can one want and yet not be unhappy if the want does not attain fulfilment? (And this possibility always exists.)
>
> Is it, according to common conceptions, good to want *nothing* for one's neighbour, neither good nor evil?
>
> And yet in a certain sense it seems that not wanting is the only good.
>
> Here I am still making crude mistakes! No doubt about that! (*NB* pp. 77–78, 29.7.16)

What are the crude mistakes? The will as ethical is still not fully understood. If to be concerned for one's neighbor is to will and if unhappiness is the necessary result of willing and not attaining, then the will that wills one's neighbor's welfare is still hostage to the world. As such, it is still an item in the world. But then it is not ethical at all. The will can be made unhappy by its survey of the world only if it wants one thing and not another and the guilt that is possible for the will as autobiographical transcendence exposes that possibility. But a will that wants one thing and not another just is a particular empirical will.

Although autobiographical transcendence offers a way to understand the claim that ethics is transcendental, it does not yield a transcendence that parallels that of the metaphysical subject. For that, we must move beyond the world as a field of action or even as an object of moral assessment. It must be confronted as an aesthetic object appreciated. But in order to prepare the way for an understanding of this aesthetic appreciation, we must first examine a number of Wittgenstein's remarks that suggest a form of stoic transcendence. I believe that stoicism does not compete with either the moral or the aesthetic as a comprehensive understanding of the good life. Rather, it prepares the way for the more complete transcendence of the aesthetic in two ways, one practical and the other theoretical. First and practically, only if one can extract oneself from the world by "renouncing the amenities of the world" (NB p. 81, 13.8.16) is aesthetic transcendence possible. In this sense the aesthetic presupposes the stoic as preparation, but at the same time aesthetic transcendence itself contains stoic renunciation as an element. Second and theoretically, much that needs to be said in order to understand Wittgenstein's stoicism prepares the way for understanding what he has in mind by aesthetic transcendence.

The Stoic

Wittgenstein's stoicism is closely linked to his understanding of the will as impotent. If the will is completely powerless, then as Wittgenstein says,

> I can only make myself independent of the world—and so in a certain sense master it—by renouncing any influence on happenings. (*NB* p. 73, 11.6.16)

But this introduces a totally new meaning for "independence." As it has been discussed, independence is a "metaphysical reality"—a necessary feature of the will's relation to the world.

The world *is* independent of my will. (*T* 6.373, my emphasis) If, as I argued, the world's independence is simply an instance of the more general logical doctrines of the *Tractatus*, it is nonsense to suggest that one can *make* oneself independent of the world.

Here Wittgenstein's notion the "life of knowledge" again provides the key to understanding. If one lives in light of what the *Tractatus* shows—if one recognizes and accepts the "metaphysical reality"—one will be independent, having renounced "any influence on happenings." But, if the will *is* powerless and yet one hopes for control over happenings and lives committed to such control, frustration is certain since all attempts to control the world are doomed to ultimate failure. Thus, "the only life that is happy is the life that can renounce the amenities of the world" (*NB* p. 81, 13.8.16). The world is an independent order of events. "That is why we have the feeling of being dependent on an alien will" (*NB* p. 74, 8.7.16). Insofar as my will seeks its fulfillment *in the world,* it is at the mercy of such an "alien will." It gives up its own distinctive power by commitment to the project of mastery within the totality of facts.

The will's proper mastery consists precisely in an achieved independence from the order of events that is the world. As Wittgenstein says, "In order to live happily I must be in agreement with the world. And that is what 'being happy' *means*" (*NB* p. 75, 8.7.16). The ethical will confronts the world as a completed totality of facts. In short, "the world is *given* to me, i.e. my will enters into the world completely from outside as into something that is already there" (*NB* p. 74, 8.7.16). I can accept what is given, in which case I am in agreement with an "alien will." But I can also "disagree" with what is. The first path is that of happiness—"that is what 'being happy' *means*." The second is the path of frustration and unhappiness.

The path of happiness is to bring one's will into "harmony with nature," to borrow a phrase from the Stoic Epictetus.[1] To seek happiness by attempting to control the course of events will ultimately fail if only at death. This is why Wittgenstein says, "Fear in the face of death is the best sign of a false, i.e. a bad, life" (*NB* p. 75, 8.7.16). Even the most charmed life, in which every desire is satisfied as a "favor granted by fate," still ends in death, and therefore one's attitude to death distinguishes those whose happiness is merely accidental from those whose happiness is ethically significant, being essentially linked to the will's own activity. For the stoic, who has mastered the world by "renouncing any influence on happenings," happiness depends solely on the will's activity and is thus independent of what happens.

Though one's own attitude toward death provides an "acid test," it does not and cannot yield an objective criterion of the happy life.

> What is the objective mark of the happy, harmonious life? Here it is again clear that there cannot be any such mark, that can be *described*.
> This mark cannot be a physical one but only a metaphysical one, a transcendental one. (*NB* p. 78, 30.7.16)

The problem is that, in the usual sense, one's attitude to death is merely a particular psychological fact. But as an empirical feature of someone's will, it cannot be a criterion of happiness. This would locate the condition for the possibility of happiness *in the world*! As we have already noted, happiness in the ethically relevant sense cannot depend on any facts about the world, including particular facts about an individual will. Any empirical, objective test—any mark "that can be described"—would bring the subject into the world and so reduces happiness to the merely empirical level. Only a "mark" that characterizes a transcendental subject—a transcendental mark —would do.

These reflections leave us with an interesting problem. If, as we have just argued, "one's attitude to death" does not refer to some empirical feature of the will, neither can death, insofar as it is ethically relevant, be an event that happens to a will. As Wittgenstein says, "At death the world does not alter, but comes to an end" (*T* 6.431). But then what does Wittgenstein mean by "death," and why does the issue arise at all? A full discussion of this issue must wait until after we have developed the notion of aesthetic transcendence, but some preliminary points can be made here.

There is a traditional way that the fear of death has been avoided. If, on metaphysical grounds, death is not ultimate, if life goes on after death, and if one's fate is guaranteed at that point by God, there need be nothing to fear. Of course, such a metaphysical account cannot meet Wittgenstein's concerns.

> Not only is there no guarantee of the temporal immortality of the human soul, that is to say of its eternal survival after death; but, in any case, this assumption completely fails to accomplish the purpose for which it has always been intended. (*T* 6.4312)

What is that purpose? This life "has meaning" because it makes a difference to what happens in the next. What I do now has meaning by contributing to some larger project that makes an eternal difference. But mere temporal duration is not the relevant issue. Wittgenstein is certainly right to say that a life that merely lasts cannot "give meaning" to one that does not. The question "What is the point of all the happiness and suffering here and now?" will simply recur for a happiness or suffering that is endless. If one enjoys uninterrupted prosperity, the fact of its continuation will not answer any questions about why it is happening.

What is important about "eternal life" is that in it one receives one's *just* reward; one's fate is connected with the absolute ethical order of things. In this life the wicked often flourish while the good flounder. As Kierkegaard so clearly saw:

> The outward world is subjected to the law of imperfection, and again and again the experience is repeated that he too who does not work gets the bread, and he who sleeps gets it more abundantly than the man who works. In the outward world everything is made payable to the bearer . . . he who has the world's treasure has it, however he got it.[2]

But in the "eternal life" to come, all this will be made right. Nothing will be accidental. Each person's fate will be necessarily connected with his or her worth. God's will and its power insure this coincidence of character and fate. The meaning of life is finally given in terms of an ethical order and one's place in it!

In God's will we are supposed to have a union of power and worth. But how are we to conceive that union, for "it is clear that ethics has nothing to do with punishment and reward in the usual sense of the terms" (T 6.422)? Here, however, "ethics" has everything to do with reward and punishment. God rewards the good and punishes the evil. And that is supposed to provide significance for all that is done here and now.

Plato clearly saw the problem when he asked if the good is good because God wills it or if it is good and that is why God wills it. If we accept the second alternative, the good is independent of God's will, and the problem of the union of power and worth is not solved. It is only God's ability to mete out reward and punishment that would be relevant for this alternative. If, on the other hand, the good is good because God wills it, then we are confronted with a cosmic tyranny of one will over all others.

Wittgenstein discusses this classic dilemma when he comments on Schlick's ethics.

> Schlick says that theological ethics contains two conceptions of the essence of the Good. According to the more superficial interpretation, the Good is good because God wills it; according to the deeper interpretation, God wills the Good because it is good.
>
> I think that the first conception is the deeper: Good is what God orders. For this cuts off the path to any and every explanation "why" it is good, while the second conception is precisely the superficial, the rationalistic one, which proceeds as if what is good could still be given some foundation. (LE p. 15)

Though Wittgenstein seems to accept the first horn of the Platonic dilemma, his real position is by no means simple. Note the parallel between Wittgenstein's comments here and his earlier discussion of the ancient and modern scientific world views. The strength of the ancient view was that it marked a clear "terminus" to explanation by appealing to "God and Fate." God, as that which is beyond understanding, stands outside all explanation. Here, in the case of value, Wittgenstein is appealing to this same feature. Those who accept the first horn of the dilemma—that what is good is good because God wills it—relinquish all further attempts to provide value any "foundation." In this way they cut off further discussion and so remain properly silent on matters about which we cannot speak. The rationalistic alternative keeps open the possibility of further discussion and so tries to "make it look as if *everything* were explained" (T 6.372).

The parallel with the earlier discussion also allows us to make a second point. By treating God as a metaphysical posit, as something that can be talked about, the ancient view destroys the very difference that it is at such pains to highlight. Similarly, if God's will is treated as a metaphysical posit, the attempt to "found" all values on God's will becomes the "cosmic tyranny" already mentioned. As an item in the world, God's will is simply one will among others that could derive authority only from its supposed power to enforce its dictates, but that is not authority at all.

There is a positive dimension to Wittgenstein's acceptance of the view that the good is good because God wills it. However, understanding that dimension requires a complete reinterpretation of "God's will." This can be provided only after we have a more detailed development of Wittgenstein's aesthetic position. Suffice it to say now that Wittgenstein's positive acceptance depends on the idea that God's will is in no sense an item in the world. Rather, he contends that

> How things stand, is God.
>
> God is, how things stand. (*NB* p. 79, 1.8.16)

God and the world are ethically one and the same. More on this later.

Given the "metaphysical God" traditionally presupposed by the Platonic dilemma, neither horn is adequate. We are still left with the fact that "When an ethical law of the form, 'Thou shalt . . .', is laid down, one's first thought is, 'And what if I do not do it?'" (*T* 6.422). The traditional metaphysical account cannot offer an adequate answer to this question since it can only appeal to God's power to enforce his will. That makes ethical value relative to a single cosmic will and so robs it of all but relative value.

For Wittgenstein the problem of death is linked directly to the will by way of living not in time but in the present. He says, "For life in the present there is no death" (*NB* p. 75, 8.7.16), and again in the *Tractatus*, "If we take eternity to mean not infinite temporal duration but timelessness, then eternal life belongs to those who live in the present" (*T* 6.4311). If one lives with the illusion of power in the world, then one lives in time in the sense that life is a bundle of plans and anticipations, hopes and fears, wishes and desires. We plan and anticipate future events, hope for or fear what may happen, and so forth. In this way, life is never complete in the present moment; what comes after makes all the difference. For such a will, immersed in the world, happiness or unhappiness is an accidental empirical phenomenon without ethical import. Desire makes us hostage to the future and makes us necessarily open to frustration, loss, and suffering. This shows up most dramatically in our relation to death, which is the final unavoidable defeat for the will that has not renounced "influence on happenings."

The will taken as an item in the world—the empirical will—must fail. But the will that "makes itself independent" by renouncing the world achieves transcendence precisely by embracing the impotence of the will. This stoic "life of knowledge" should be carefully distinguished from another stance, which can be called "naive prudence." The latter proceeds from a simple lack of awareness of the "true condition of the will." Here the agent unreflectively pursues a life within the realm of happenings. Such a life may be characterized by practical wisdom or folly, and some form of stoicism may play a role by counseling acceptance as a wise strategy for getting on in the world. However, this can be of no interest to Wittgenstein. Such a life happens in a "pre-ethical" context since the agent has not achieved the perspective of the ethical subject from which the world is confronted as a whole. There is no possibility of ethical value at all. Whether one is happy or unhappy, in such a life nothing of ethical significance can occur. But, and this is the point with which this discussion of death began, there can be no objective mark in terms of which one can determine that "happy life" which proceeds from ethical transcendence and that which is merely the result of naive prudence.

Of course, there is a third alternative. Suppose that there is recognition of the will's impotence but that this is denied, found unacceptable, or otherwise rejected. Unhappiness—being in "disagreement with the world"—is now built into the very fabric of the will's relation to the world. The basis of such unhappiness is not any item in the world; it is that there is a world—an alien will—over against mine. It is in this way that the world of the unhappy person is an unhappy world. That unhappiness that has ethical import is as distinct from the unhappiness that merely befalls an empirical will— through a failure of naive prudence—as ethical happiness is from its empirical counterpart.

In this there is something analogous to the existential notion of "bad faith." There is the attempt to avoid responsibility for the world by refusing to accept the ethical condition of the will. Here, the popular notion of responsibility that depends on the idea that "there are things that I do, and other things not done by me" (*NB* p. 88, 4.11.16) may come into play. The attempt is to limit ethical responsibility to a specific range of acts so that one can be said to have carried out "one's responsibilities." Such a view depends essentially on suppressing the necessity of ethical transcendence and by so doing identifies the ethical subject as a particular empirical self. But, as Wittgenstein says in another context, and as has been shown here, the philosophical and ethical "self is not the human being, not the human body, or the human soul with which psychology deals (*T* 5.641). Rather, it is the "metaphysical subject [taken as will for ethics], the limit of the world—not a part of it" (*T* 5.641). Bad faith for Wittgenstein is simply the attempt to suppress the implications of the transcendence of the will. It is to be contrasted with naive prudence for which the will's transcendence is neither explicitly or implicitly presupposed. Naive prudence is pre-ethical, but bad faith is an ethical position because it essentially involves a recognition of the will's relation to the world as a totality, but at the same time it attempts to hide, ignore, or otherwise suppress that recognition.

The stoicism that is developed here presupposes the transcendence of the will in two ways. First, it presupposes the "metaphysical condition of the will"—the world *is* independent of my will. Second, it presupposes the recognition *and* acceptance of that condition. Stoic happiness or unhappiness is, then, a function of "my attitude" to the condition of the will (*NB* p. 87, 4.11.16). It is just this duality that explains the two senses of "independence" with which we began. The ethical subject as the necessary condition of the possibility of ethical value *is* independent, and the ethical subject as that which lives the happy life, wills that independence, and so appropriates it to itself, becomes independent.

This duality, which is essential to stoic transcendence, also makes it impossible to take it as a free-standing complete position within Wittgenstein's thought. It opens it to a fatal objection, for there is an important ambiguity in the idea of an "empirical will." On the one hand, that term refers to a will engaged in the project to influence happenings and is therefore contrasted with a will that has "transcended the world" in the sense that it has abandoned that project. But on the other hand, the term refers to a will that is an item in the world—a particular will. An empirical will in the second sense need not be one in the first. In fact, only a will that is an item in the world can "transcend the world" by renouncing the project of influencing happenings. Renouncing that project is, after all, something that is done by some individuals but not others and at some times but perhaps not at others, and so on. This means that stoic transcendence, taken by itself, is open to an objection similar to that raised against the moral level. Insofar as stoic happiness is achieved, it can have only relative value. That achievement is a fact about a particular will in the world and, as we have said before, "in the world no value exists and if it did exist it would have no value." Therefore stoicism, taken by itself, involves a confusion between a limited psychological transcendence and logical transcendence. It cannot yield the notion of the ethical subject so essential to Wittgenstein's contention that "ethics is transcendental."

Perhaps the stoic is merely a preparatory stage in and through which one comes to the true appropriation of the world. Most individuals never confront the world as a totality and so remain at the pre-ethical level of naive prudence. Others do see the world as a whole and so reach the level of the ethical but cannot or do not will the world as it is and so are unhappy. Stoic renunciation can allow one to see the world as a totality, but what is the nature of the willing in which my will becomes the world will? It is not mere stoic acceptance of what is, but something more positive. It is the aesthetic appreciation of the world in which the final union of self and world occurs.

The Aesthetic

In the *Tractatus* Wittgenstein says, "Ethics and aesthetics are one and the same" (*T* 6.421), but there he gives no further assistance in understanding that claim. Fortunately, in the *Notebooks* there is a very revealing passage. "The work of art is the object seen *sub specie aeternitatis;* and the good life is the world seen *sub specie aeternitatis.* This is the connexion between art and ethics" (*NB* p. 83, 7.10.16). But what is it to see an object *sub specie aeternitatis?* Perhaps we can get at this by first focusing on our practical concern for things around us. Wittgenstein says, "The usual way of looking at things sees objects as it were from the midst of them" (*NB* p. 83, 7.10.16). Consider, for example, a paper cup. It is merely something that can contain a liquid so that its properties are totally determined by that end and its value depends on its capacity to serve immediate or future interest. As a mere means to particular ends, one cup is as good as another. We pay no attention to an individual object's intrinsic features. Rather, we "see right through it" to the purpose that it serves. Clearly, for Wittgenstein, such things have only relative value. They are certainly not "seen *sub specie aeternitatis*." Rather they are items-in-the-world caught up in the flux and flow of events, available to serve or frustrate the interests of particular empirical wills.

By contrast, part of what it is to see a work of art as a work of art is to suspend our usual practical concern.[3] This is brought out very clearly by some pieces of contemporary art. Consider such works as Christo's "Running Fence" or John Cage's "Silences." "Silences" aims at getting us to suspend our usual attitude to the everyday noises around us. Whereas typically these sounds serve us as cues for action, in the concert hall we are to pay attention to the intrinsic character of the sounds themselves. Similarly, by constructing a "fence" that cuts across open country, our everyday practical concern is called into question. What was merely a field under cultivation arrests our attention. The intrinsic shapes, colors, and textures of the landscape are made accessible to us.

By placing ordinary objects in an aesthetic context—in a gallery, for example—one suspends their immediate practical roles. Perhaps this is nowhere more apparent than with normal utilitarian objects—utensils, textiles, and pottery—that are offered for aesthetic appreciation. As presented for aesthetic enjoyment, they are not available for use. It is just the gallery's ability to cancel or objectify our usual attitudes and expectations that brings about the "transformation" of everyday items into works of art. Offered for aesthetic appreciation, a pottery bowl is not available for use. Its actual utility in the "real" world is held in suspension as the object is frozen in time. Its aesthetic features are just those it has, here and now, isolated from the viewer's practical concerns. In this sense it is a completed totality, given once and for all. It is given *sub specie aeternitatis*.

More traditional works of art also bear out these points. A painting is not a field for action. Its space is not continuous with the actual space around it. It is not (except accidentally) even a map or guide to the nature or character of some part of the world. The space *in* the painting and the space in which the painting is viewed are essentially external to each other. The work of art occurs in the space of the viewer, but the viewer is not in the space of the painting. As a result, as viewers we are not agents in any usual sense at all. We do not engage aesthetic objects as available for use as we do a telephone or a paper cup. Although these ordinary objects occupy the same field that we do and are available to interact with us in various ways, we are set over against the painting as spectators. Each work of art is given—as a totality—to be appreciated or enjoyed, not acted upon.

The relationship between objects available for everyday concern and objects aesthetically apprehended is laid out by Wittgenstein in the following passage.

> As a thing among things, each thing is equally insignificant; as a world each one equally significant.
>
> If I have been contemplating the stove, and then am told: but now all you know is the stove, my result does indeed seem trivial. For this represents the matter as if I had studied the stove as one among the many things in the world. But if I was contemplating the stove *it* was my world, and everything else colourless by contrast with it.
>
> (Something good about the whole, but bad in details.)
>
> For it is equally possible to take the bare present image as the worthless momentary picture in the whole temporal world, and as the true world among shadows. (*NB* p. 83, 8.10.16)

Notice that there are "two stoves." There is the stove-among-other-things, the knowledge of which is said to be trivial. If the stove is a single item in a sea of other items, even a complete knowledge of the stove (whatever that might be) would amount to nothing. But there is also the stove-as-my-world against which everything else is colorless. The stove-as-my-world is an aesthetic object to be appreciated, contemplated, and "enjoyed," where enjoyment does not have a utilitarian overtone. All practical interests have been suspended so the object no longer takes its value from its capacities to satisfy particular needs. It is intrinsically interesting.

The whole world can occur for me in the way that the stove-as-my-world occurs, and that is "the good life." There are "two worlds." There is the world that is the mere aggregate of facts, that is to say, a collection of facts among other facts, within which each fact is "equally insignificant." In the world everything simply is as it is; in it no value exists (*T* 6.41). But there is also the world-as-the-totality-of-facts, the whole seen as a whole *sub specie aeternitatis*. That is *my world*. That is the world viewed from without, as an aesthetic object appreciated.

What would it mean to see the world in this aesthetic way—*sub specie aeternitatis*? So viewed, the world—the totality of facts—is simply given for appreciation. It is not a field for action or judgment, and there is no desire to be fulfilled or frustrated by subsequent events. The richness of detail is taken for itself, not, as it would be for an empirically situated agent, as a cue for action. In fact, the subject of this experience is not an item in the experienced field. As with the painting, the viewer stands over against what it experiences, which, in this case, is the world.

For the subject that aesthetically transcends the world, there is no acceptance or rejection, simply appreciation. To take a phrase from another part of the *Tractatus*, the "subject shrinks to a point without extension, and there remains the reality co-ordinate with it" (*T* 5.64). However, that reality is not the "colorless" totality of facts; it is the "aesthetically appreciated" totality apprehended by a pure will that has achieved the perspective of the metaphysical subject. As a will, it becomes identical with the "metaphysical subject" that is the logical limit of the world and representation. Just as the metaphysical subject "shrinks to a point without extension," the ethical subject "disappears" in this achievement, for it no longer constitutes an independent I over against the world so that what remains is simply the-totality-of-facts aesthetically appreciated.

As aesthetic transcendence, my will escapes all the contingencies of the world, and so its happiness is solely a function of its identity with the world. This is how the aesthetic escapes the problems that Wittgenstein found with the moral stage. Recall that he asks whether it is possible to will good, to will evil, and not to will and concludes that not willing is the only good (*NB* p. 77, 29.7.16). But at the moral level there is, as the analysis of guilt clearly shows, still an unavoidable component of willing. This is finally left behind in the aesthetic since there, nothing in particular is willed. The totality of fact as a totality is aesthetically appreciated so that what is willed is in necessary agreement with what is. This is what makes for the identity of the metaphysical subject of the logical doctrines and the willing subject of the ethical. Wittgenstein says, "as my idea is the world, in the same way my will is the world-will" (*NB* p. 85, 17.10.16).

Remember how it is that the world is my world. The world that is represented in language is, of course, represented by my language, which as language is "the only language." So the world and the world represented by me—my world—are one and the same. The world is my world. The world is the totality of facts, and every idea is a representation of an actual or possible fact. So the limits of representation—of my idea—just are the limits of what is represented—the world. So my idea, taken simply as the possibility of representation, just is the world taken as what is capable of being represented. The important point to remember is that the "idea" that is "my idea" is mine merely in the sense that it is a possible thought and so a possible thought of mine. As an idea, as a representation of the world, it is in no sense unique to me. In the *Tractatus* Wittgenstein attempts to specify the limits of all possible thought and by so doing to specify the limits of "my thought," so it is just when everything that pertains to me as a particular individual is deleted from "my idea" that it is true that "my idea is the world." This, as we have seen, is the essence of Wittgenstein's treatment of solipsism. The subject for which the world is—the metaphysical subject—is language taken as the possibility of representation. And that subject shrinks to a point without extension.

How can this also be true for "my will?" How can my will be the world-will? If "my will" is taken to be an idiosyncratic, individual will, such a claim would be analogous to metaphysical solipsism, in which case the world would be mysteriously dependent on a particular will, which is absurd since any particular will is merely an item in the world. On the other hand, if "my will" refers to the possibility of willing in which what is and what is willed are essentially identical, that is to say, a situation in which everything idiosyncratic is removed from my will, then what I will and what is—the totality of facts—will be the same. My will is the world-will. Of course, when my will wills the totality of facts, it does not will a particular actual totality; it wills whatever happens to be the totality simply by virtue of its being the totality. So the will that is the world-will is the will of the ethical subject, just as the idea that is the "world idea" is the idea of the metaphysical subject.

We can finally see what Wittgenstein really meant when he said that ethics and aesthetics are one (T 6.421). He did not mean that they are simply the same in form or that "judgment" in ethics has the same logical standing as "judgment" in aesthetics. This is certainly what the positivists took him to mean, but true or not, it does not go to the heart of the matter. Rather, at the highest level, the good life—the happy life—consists of an aesthetic apprehension and appreciation of the world in which will and idea are an essential unity. The metaphysical subject and the willing ethical subject are one and the same.

The essential unity of Wittgenstein's philosophical vision is fully evident. Seeing the world rightly—seeing what the *Tractatus* shows —is, on the side of idea, what willing the world rightly—willing the totality shown in the *Tractatus*—is on the side of will. And since Wittgenstein insists that it is not possible to "conceive a being that isn't capable of Will at all, but only of Idea" (*NB* p. 77, 14.7.16), "the world and life are one" (*T* 5.621). The logical and ethical aspects of the early Wittgenstein's thought are unified in the essential unity of will and idea. That is exactly why he can say of the *Tractatus* that "the book's point is an ethical one." To apprehend the world as the totality of facts is to be brought to a wordless appreciation of that totality, and so the vision that opens the work brings us, when appreciated, to the silence that ends it.

For the metaphysical subject and, as we have now seen, for the ethical will, the world is given complete as a totality. For such a subject, one that apprehends the world *sub specie aeternitatis*, there can be no change since all change is already contained in the object contemplated. Each moment of aesthetic contemplation is complete. This provides a new opening on Wittgenstein's various comments on death. Consider first the comments in the *Tractatus* that "at death the world does not alter, but comes to an end" (*T* 6.431) and that "death is not an event in life: we do not live to experience death" (*T* 6.4311). What Wittgenstein means here is connected directly to his analysis of the ethical will, and this is made clear by noting that both of these passages are comments on *Tractatus* 6.43, where Wittgenstein says that the world of the happy person is a different world from that of the unhappy person. It is the world of the happy or unhappy person that comes to an end with death. But as the previous discussion shows, that just is the world.

Let us review several points. In a passage discussed earlier, Wittgenstein says that if the will did not exist, neither would there be a center to the world. What does he mean? First, consider the claim in relation to the logical or metaphysical aspects of the *Tractatus*. If there were no I—no metaphysical subject—there would be no *totality* of facts since the collection of facts taken individually would not be "gathered up" into a totality. But "the world is the *totality* of facts" (*T* 1.1). So for there to be "the world," there must be that gathering up into a whole that is implicit in the idea of the metaphysical subject. Without that, and here language really does fail, there would be a mere "heap" of individual facts. But, of course, the very possibility of entertaining that suggestion requires us to reject it since as represented, that is, thought, it already presupposes the metaphysical subject. The world without individual consciousnesses —empirical subjects—is perfectly conceivable (or we might say that its inconceivability is a *mere* empirical matter), but the world without the metaphysical subject is unrepresentable and so unthinkable.

Now remember that, as we have just seen, Wittgenstein rejects the notion that we can conceive a being that is capable of idea but not of will (*NB* p. 77, 24.7.16). But this means that the metaphysical subject is also and essentially will. So to remove the I is to remove the world as ethical domain. But the world as ethical domain just is the world, that is, the totality of facts occurring as a totality.

But now what can "death" mean, given all this? Death is the cessation of life, but "the World and Life are one" and "physiological life is of course not 'Life'. And neither is psychological life. Life is the world" (*NB* p. 77, 24.7.16). Remember that the metaphysical subject is "not the human body [physiological life] or the human soul [psychological life] . . . but . . . the limit of the world." Further, "Ethics must be a condition of the world, like logic" (*NB* p. 77, 24.7.16). The ethical subject is also the logical limit of the world but as willable, not as representable. Of course, these are one and the same, for they are both the totality of fact. Death would then be the absence of the conditions for the possibility of ethical willing. The absence of the metaphysical subject is unrepresentable since its "presence" is presupposed by and "shown" in every representation. So the absence of the ethical subject is unrepresentable. Death is not an occurrence in the world. Just as the metaphysical subject is the world taken from the point of view of representation so that the medium of representation disappears or "shrinks to a point without extension," so the ethical subject is the possibility of willing the world in which the will disappears or "shrinks to a point without extension." This occurs in aesthetic transcendence. Now, if there were no will—no ethical subject—there would be no life and so no world. At death the world simply comes to an end. There is no more world of the happy or unhappy person.

This leads to Wittgenstein's remarks on death that connect it with happiness.

> A man who is happy must have no fear not even in the face of death.
> Only a man who lives not in time but in the present is happy.
> For life in the present there is no death. (*NB* pp. 74–75, 8.7.16)

We have already commented on these remarks from the point of view of stoic transcendence, but their meaning is enriched by the aesthetic. The basic argument is clear enough. The happy person is one who lives in the present, and for such a one there is no death. So the happy person can have no fear of death since it does not even exist for him or her. But what does Wittgenstein mean by "living in the present," and why is there no death for such a one? Wittgenstein says, "If we take eternity to mean not infinite temporal duration but timelessness, then eternal life belongs to those who live in the present" (*T* 6.4311). For the stoic, living in the present only has the negative sense of "renouncing control over happenings," but for the ethical subject as aesthetic transcendence, it involves the positive appropriation of the totality of facts as an aesthetic object. The world occurs complete in the present moment for aesthetic transcendence which experiences the totality of facts *sub specie aeternitatis* so that there is only the present—the moment in which the world is apprehended as aesthetic object. But such a moment obviously need not and does not possess infinite temporal duration. Rather, the point is that from within it there is no temporal differentiation so that internally it is timeless. That is what it means to say that the world is given as a whole—as a *totality of facts*. Such a moment can come to an end, but that "is not an event *in* life." It is not an occurrence within that eternity, which is living in the present. So "at death the world [of the happy person] does not alter, but comes to an end" (*T* 6.431).

Death and the Silence of the *Tractatus*

As we now see, Wittgenstein's ethical theory involves a rejection of autobiographical transcendence in favor of stoic acceptance as a condition of and an element in the aesthetic for which the world is no longer a field of action or moral judgment but is an aesthetic object to be contemplated. The similarities with Schopenhauer's ethical views are certainly pervasive and striking. It appears, however, that Wittgenstein has reversed the priority of what Schopenhauer called the saintly and the aesthetic. Whereas Schopenhauer contends that the aesthetic offers only a transient escape from the will that is ultimately inferior to the saintly life, Wittgenstein sees the aesthetic as the very height of human existence.

However, the discussion to this point exposes two distinct problems for the moral level (and for the stoic, if it is treated as another independent possibility). In the first place, since for autobiographical transcendence it is possible to be either happy or unhappy and since happiness or unhappiness cannot be a function of the way the world is, each must be a function of some difference in the subject for which the world is either happy or unhappy. But any such difference forces us to understand the subject as an item in the world and so makes it impossible to treat it as transcendental. And this is a formal feature of autobiographical transcendence since guilt is an essential possibility for it.

If stoic transcendence is treated, as I have treated it here, as preparatory to and an element in aesthetic transcendence, it, along with aesthetic transcendence, avoids this problem. For aesthetic transcendence all difference is overcome. Aesthetic appreciation just is an appreciation of the world as the totality of facts. For it, there is no room for unhappiness. For ordinary aesthetic experience there is always the possibility of finding an object uninteresting, ugly, or otherwise deficient, and this would seem to correspond to unhappiness for the moral level. However, this possibility arises just because ordinary aesthetic experience concerns particular objects that might be different in specific ways. But insofar as one's aesthetic appreciation depends on an object's being one way as opposed to another, the transcendence appropriate to the ethical simply has not yet been achieved. For aesthetic vision that appropriates the totality of facts as the totality of facts, there can be no ugliness. The totality of facts is not appreciated because it is *this* totality but because it is *the* totality of facts.

However, this still leaves a second problem. In every case, including the aesthetic, happiness is an achievement. It is, after all, a matter of recognizing and appropriating the independence of the will. But any such achievement must be an event in the world that happens to some specifiable individual. As such, it can have no absolute value, for again, "In the world everything is as it is, and everything happens as it does happen: *in* it no value exists—and if it did exist, it would have no value" (*T* 6.41). But this creates a certain paradox because that which is of absolute value is, when achieved, devoid of value. The good life cannot be lived and retain its value!

The very plausibility of Wittgenstein's account of the good life depends on confusing forms of psychological transcendence with the apparent logical transcendence of the metaphysical subject. In this way he is able to treat individual wills as transcendental. The difficulty here comes sharply into focus if we reconsider Wittgenstein's discussions of living in the present and death.

Consider first his discussion of death. Why does the issue arise at all? If, in fact, Wittgenstein is discussing the logical conditions for the possibility of absolute or ethical value, what has death to do with the matter? Logical conditions do not die! Doesn't the very fact that Wittgenstein raises the issue suggest that he is thinking about particular individuals? Doesn't it suggest that when he says that the world of the happy person is a different world from that of the unhappy person, he has in mind particular individuals who will the world differently? But, as we have seen, if the happy person is a particular individual, then that happiness has no ethical value.

Perhaps the force of this objection can be avoided along the following lines. Ethics requires the *possibility* of willing the world. However, that possibility does not require the existence of any particular will. Nor does it require that some particular will exist. All that it requires is the possibility of particular wills. But such a possibility is a logical, not empirical, matter and so is given prior to all truth or falsity—that is, prior to any actual way the world is, including its containing some particular wills. Thus, to talk of an ethical will is merely to talk of a possibility of willing the world as a totality and so is not to talk of any actual will.

Suppose all this is correct; it only brings us back to the question of the meaning of death. So long as the discussion proceeds at the level here considered, there seems no room for such an issue, and the very attempt to raise it betrays a shift. Death can only be the loss of the possibility of willing the world. But what can that mean except that a particular will that did exist no longer exists, and, of course, that is an event in the world. Even the more radical possibility of the death of all particular wills is but an event or set of events in the world—a *mere* empirical possibility.

The fact that Wittgenstein raises the issue of death at all suggests that he has illicitly—from his own point of view—run together the two notions of empirical will and ethical subject. The happy person is, then, any individual will that has achieved a particular attitude to the world. This can be made clearer by distinguishing two quite distinct senses of "an individual will." On the one hand, that term might be used to refer to a will that is distinguished from another by reference to some difference in content. That is, for one will there is something that it wills that the other does not. Clearly, the happy person as aesthetic transcendence is not individual in this sense since happiness is achieved precisely by eliminating all content that is idiosyncratic. Let us call a will that is individuated by content a qualitatively individual will so that the ethical subject is *essentially* not a qualitatively individual will. However, there is a second sense of "individual" that underlies the very characterization of qualitative individuality. After all, to talk of two wills that share the same content is already to presuppose at least logically distinct wills. Given this distinction, we can say that the happy person is a particular logically individual will that is not qualitatively individual since it wills the world as an aesthetically appreciated totality.

With this in mind, we can see why it makes perfect sense for Wittgenstein to introduce the topic of death as he does, and we can understand what he has to say. The world as "the world of the happy man"—the world as *aesthetically appreciated*—simply comes to an end with the death of that logically individual will. There is no longer a willing and so there is no longer what is willed, which, in this case, is the world aesthetically appropriated. But, of course, this locates the happy person in the world, at least from the logical point of view, even though the happy person transcends the world in the way the world is willed. Logically the happy person is merely an item in the world, but psychologically the happy person transcends the world.

The same equivocation is present in Wittgenstein's discussion of "living in the present." The attempt to distinguish eternity as infinite temporal duration from eternity as timelessness commits us to two perspectives on a single event. Insofar as living in the present lacks infinite temporal duration, it is an event that lasts for a determinate time and is preceded and followed by other events. In short, it is one event among others in the world. However, seen from within as the experience of the totality of facts, there is no temporal differentiation and so there is timelessness.

The notion of the present moment does not arise for aesthetic transcendence, understood in its own terms. To identify a moment as the present moment is to locate it in terms of other moments, some of which are past and others future but all of which are not contained in the current moment of apprehension. In short, it is to stand outside that moment and to see it as one moment among many. For aesthetic apprehension, the contemplated object—the totality of facts—does not occur at a moment. It includes all moments. For this reason, talk of "the present" is strictly inappropriate here. For aesthetic transcendence there is no present, past, or future. These are terms borrowed from that discourse which marks differences within the world but which have no application to the world as the totality of facts. Of course, given the general account of language developed in the *Tractatus*, everything that can be said can be said in that discourse. Wittgenstein seems to have "run up against the limits of language" here, and at the same time he has run up against the limits of the ethical. Insofar as the eternal is without "infinite temporal duration," it is one moment among others and so is located within the world and therefore loses its ethical status. And it is Wittgenstein's own attempt to draw the relevant distinction that drives us to this conclusion.

Wittgenstein's failure to confront this problem is connected with his doctrine of showing. As we have seen, that doctrine is designed to make philosophically accessible what cannot be said. That is, it is supposed to make it possible to find a place for what cannot be said within Wittgenstein's thinking without violating the fundamental account of meaning he develops. At the same time, of course, it allows Wittgenstein a place for his ethical *thinking*, but does it make room for the ethical life? We have found that the ethical life lived necessarily becomes an item in the world, at least in the logical sense. And as such, it loses its ethical value. But in a certain sense the same is true of the perspective of the metaphysical subject—grasped, it becomes a view of a particular subject and so reduces itself to an item in the world. That is why on the logical side the strictly correct procedure would be to merely carry on with science, that is, to say what can be said against the backdrop of the silence that the *Tractatus* provides. What is the parallel move on the ethical side? It is to merely proceed with life (after all, everything in the world remains the same) but against the backdrop of Tractarian silence in terms of which the everyday affairs of life are thrown into aesthetic relief. But "Tractarian silence" is by no means *mere* silence, and this point only shifts the focus of problem to silence itself. Tractarian silence is not and cannot be a silence-in-the-world. It is a silence *about* the world taken as a totality. All the problems about the possibility of ethical living simply reassert themselves in this problem of silence, which will be discussed in detail shortly.

Both strands of the previous discussion suggest that Wittgenstein must have in mind *particular* experiences that have a certain psychological structure. To talk of living in the present or of death is to locate a particular moment in relation to other moments, and this is to locate the happiness of the happy person in the world. But as such, no moment can have absolute value. Thus we seem to be committed, insofar as we would preserve the absolute value of achieved happiness, to treating an individual subject as the "ethical subject" and so as transcendental subject. Unfortunately, this, as I will argue in the next chapters, compromises the entire account of the metaphysical subject and transcendence that underlies the *Tractatus*.

7

THE TENSION BETWEEN ETHICAL

AND LOGICAL TRANSCENDENCE

Logic and Ethics

In its logical sense transcendence cannot be an attitude that a particular subject takes to the rest of the world. That is, it cannot be seen as an achievement of a particular subject. Whatever happens for or to a particular empirical subject is among the totality of facts and so can be represented by language. But Wittgenstein insists that the transcendence of the metaphysical subject cannot be represented. It is not an item in the world. The idea that it can both constitute the limit of all possible representation and be represented is solipsism in its metaphysical form. Wittgenstein's whole account of philosophical subjectivity is designed to overcome this confusion.

Such a notion of transcendence, totally inadequate to the logical doctrines of the *Tractatus*, is illustrated and rejected by Wittgenstein when he says,

For the form of the visual field is surely not like this

$(T\ 5.6331)$.

The problem with this picture is that the eye is located *in* it. But if the eye is a part of the picture, then its being so presupposes an eye that finds it (the first eye) within the picture, and that eye (the second eye) cannot be a part of the picture. It is a necessary condition of there being a picture. This is what Wittgenstein means when he says that nothing *in* the visual field allows one to infer that it is seen. But as we have already pointed out, we can infer that it is seen from there being a *visual field* at all. Thus the metaphysical subject "does not belong to the world: rather, it is a limit of the world" (*T* 5.632).

It is precisely transcendence in this rejected sense that is involved in each of the levels discussed in the previous chapter. Although it is correct to see the stoic as transcending the world in a certain way, it is also true that the stoic will is a particular will very much in the world. To use the language of the phenomenologists, we might say that the stoic will is a particular way of "being-in-the-world," one that is structured by a kind of attitude to the world. Similarly, the moral level does not involve absolute or logical transcendence at all. Rather, as we have already seen, it is a particular attitude of the self with regard to itself and the rest of the world. However, it is an attitude of a particular type very much in the world. And of course, the same holds even for the aesthetic level.

Now, Wittgenstein conceives of the transcendence implicit in the ethical as identical with that of the metaphysical subject. In fact, at the aesthetic level the ethical will becomes identical with the metaphysical subject so that "as my idea is the world, in the same way my will is the world-will" (*NB* p. 85, 17.10.16). But that is exactly the problem. If happiness is achieved, then the transcendence of the ethical subject must be accessible to particular situated wills. In that case it cannot be transcendence in the metaphysical sense at all. It must be understood as an attitude open to particular subjects in the world not as a perspective that strictly speaking encompasses the whole. But, the form of this sort of transcendence is precisely that rejected at *T* 5.6331, discussed above.

Can this equivocation on the notion of transcendence be avoided within the context of the project of the *Tractatus*? Let us reexamine the basis on which subjectivity was introduced into the *Tractatus*. As we saw, a state of affairs and a state of affairs as representing are logically distinct, even though every proposition is itself a state of affairs. The criteria of identity for each are distinct, and to speak of representation is to speak of what happens for subjectivity. Without subjectivity there would be an inarticulated mass of facts. However, this does not commit us to there being a subject that is both an item in the world and a condition of the possibility of all representation. Subjectivity as representable is what we have called the empirical subject and is identified by criteria that already presuppose subjectivity as the condition of the possibility of representation —the metaphysical subject. This is the import of the previous discussion of the eye and the visual field. The metaphysical subject is not any actual subject, but simply language taken in its totality as representing.

Can this sort of account be extended to the willing ethical subject? If so, there is no need to treat a particular subject as a limit of the world either logically or ethically. All that is actually involved are different criteria of identity. Consider an analogy. If we take a painting strictly as an item in the world, then it is simply a particular arrangement of paint spots on canvas, and this is not an aesthetic object. It is not even a painting except in the most trivial sense. On the other hand, as a painting, as an aesthetic object, it is a depiction of, say, ships in the harbor. Now the point is that the criteria in virtue of which something is an item-in-the-world and an aesthetic object are different so that an aesthetic object has properties that a mere item-in-the-world does not and, logically, cannot have. On this view the "aesthetic subject" is merely subjectivity considered in relation to the aesthetic object. Roughly, we might say that the aesthetic subject is a point of view open to anyone from which an object has its aesthetic properties. The aesthetic subject is the logical co-relative of the aesthetic object.

One can describe a "painting" in complete objective detail. One can even describe the art viewer viewing the painting as a sociologist or psychologist might. For such a description "aesthetic appreciation" is merely a psychological occurrence that has no absolute value. On the other hand, aesthetic appreciation as it is characterized in the language of aesthetics itself is not a mere psychological phenomenon. What cannot be captured in objective descriptions is the art viewer's own view of the painting or the object as object for the art viewer. Such "elements" are necessarily left out of any complete description of the world as the totality of facts. However, there is no vicious duplicity here, and there is no problem. Of course, the aesthetic subject is not a real subject—not an item in the world—but all that means is that a description of the aesthetic subject is not a description of some particular individual. A catalogue of the totality of facts will not include the aesthetic subject, nor will it include any aesthetic object, but, by the same token, no *fact* will be left out. The difference between an empirical subject and the aesthetic subject, then, is built into the difference between the painting as spots of paint and the painting as aesthetic object.

This seems to offer a clear avenue for understanding ethical subjectivity without confusing it with a particular will. The ethical subject is the co-relative of the totality of facts as ethical object—as object of the will. Now, just as aesthetic appreciation described as an item in the world has no value, happiness or guilt as feelings of particular individuals will have no value. But happiness as "willing the totality" characterizes, not particular subjects (except accidentally), but the ethical subject. Of course, the perspective of the ethical subject is open to anyone, just as is the aesthetic, but we cannot confuse "descriptions" from that perspective with descriptions of facts, just as we cannot confuse an aesthetic description with one in terms of items in the world. (The scare quotation marks around "descriptions," of course, arise from the *Tractatus*'s own account of saying, which leaves no room for anything that can be called a "description" of the ethical. This is simply another version of the problem we have discussed concerning whether the *Tractatus* can take account of itself.)

This interpretation offers a number of interesting insights into important aspects of the *Tractatus*. For example, it allows us to see exactly why it is that in the world no value exists. An item-in-the-world can have no aesthetic properties since it makes no sense to raise aesthetic questions about a mere collection of paint spots. From that point of view, objects simply are what they are, and there is no logical room for aesthetic appreciation or evaluation. Insofar as anything is "in the world," it can have no value. Value is excluded by the very criteria of identity that constitute the objects. There is a logical mistake—a level confusion—involved in identifying an object as an item-in-the-world and attributing value to it.

As powerful and helpful as this line of thought may be, it cannot be used to save the project of the *Tractatus* in either its ethical or logical dimensions. The reason is simple. It requires us to treat the difference between the world as the object of the ethical subject and the world as the totality of facts as a difference that depends on what it is possible to say within a particular discourse. The limits of intelligibility will be the particular limits of such a discourse, not the absolute limits of all possible discourses.

The power of the *Tractatus*, of its claim that ethics cannot be put into words, for example, derives in part from an implicit priority of the perspective of the metaphysical subject. After all, the world is the totality of facts. It is not the totality of "aesthetic facts" or the totality of "ethical facts." In some sense the facts—the world for the metaphysical subject—are neutral and prior to the ethical or aesthetic. However, once we treat the limits of "saying" in terms of what it is possible to say within a particular discourse, it will no longer be possible to give a particular discourse the sort of privileged place that the language of the totality of facts—the language of science—has for the *Tractatus*. Put another way, we can no longer claim that ethics cannot be put into words. We can only claim that it cannot be put into words that yield a particular "objective" picture of the world. Of course, this is not a very interesting claim since it amounts to saying that ethics cannot be put into words that leave no room for ethics.

If we follow out the line of defense we have been developing, we must either abandon the sharp division between "the facts" and "the value of the world" and with it the purely objective notion of fact, or we must allow for a multiplicity of discourses, no one of which is privileged. If we take the latter route, we can preserve the Tractarian notion of fact, but only as one among many possible ways of presenting the world, not as somehow definitive of the world. On both alternatives, what is lost is "the world," which acts as an anchor for Wittgenstein's whole discussion of the ethical.

Although a multiplicity of discourses may yield some notion of transcendence, it should be clear that that transcendence is itself situated, that is to say, is an item in the world in the Tractarian sense. Each particular discourse is located within a larger collection of discourses. It stands in various relations to this larger diversity, and these relations are themselves describable within yet other discourses. On the logical side, this means that we must replace the notion of "limit" as it figures in the *Tractatus* with the notion of a "situated limit," but this simply dissolves the very project of the *Tractatus*. It will no longer make sense to talk of setting the a priori limits of all possible representation. Every setting of limits will be situated within a limited horizon and possible only in virtue of that. On the ethical side, such a situated transcendence will be one among many possible stances. That is, it will be an *attitude* toward the world that is at the same time in the world. As such, it can support only what within the *Tractatus* be trivial or relative value claims. If there is only "situated transcendence," there is no ethical value. The ethical subject must lie absolutely beyond the world, for if it is an item in the world in any sense, all value would be relative value and so there would be no ethical value.

This way of setting the problem continues to preserve the distinction between absolute and relative value. But, of course, that distinction as it is developed in the *Tractatus* presupposes the notion of world that is undercut by the approach that we are examining here. The point that I am making here is that within the project of the *Tractatus*, the attempted defense destroys the absoluteness of ethical transcendence and by so doing makes ethical value in the full Tractarian sense impossible.

Although it may be reasonable to characterize the three levels that we have distinguished as modes of "transcendence," it is a simple equivocation to treat them as any more than analogically related to the notion of transcendence developed in the logical parts of the *Tractatus*. For transcendence to do its proper work in the theory of language, it must be taken simply as the limit to the possibility of all description. However, if it is to have its proper role in the ethical theory, it cannot be taken in that way. Transcendence must be seen as something that happens to and for a particular subject in the midst of things. Of course, being in the midst of things in this way is not incompatible with "standing over against the world" in the various ways that we have identified.

The problem can be put as a dilemma. Either ethics is not transcendental, in which case ethical value does not exist, for "in the world no value exists or if it did exist, it would have no value." Or if ethics is transcendental, then the metaphysical and ethical subject is one subject among others that in the context of the *Tractatus* yields solipsism of the metaphysical sort. That is, it yields a solipsism in which a particular subject is given pride of place. "The world is my world" comes to mean that it is M. H.'s world. But that is clearly absurd. So either solipsism cannot be refuted or ethics is impossible. Within the structure of the *Tractatus* there is no middle position. The attempt to take it seriously as an ethical work forces one to reject its logical doctrines, and vice versa.

There is, of course, a middle position, but it requires the rejection of the project of the *Tractatus* for, as we have seen, it involves the rejection of the notion of transcendence that defines that project. Without the transcendental perspective of the metaphysical subject, the notion of the "limit of all possible description" loses its absoluteness so that the limit is always a function of where one stands in the world. But this relativized notion of limit is antithetical to the very project of the *Tractatus*. Wittgenstein himself describes the project in clear and straightforward terms in the *Philosophical Investigations*. The task is to present

> an order, in fact the *a priori* order of the world: that is, the order of possibilities, which must be common to both world and thought. But this order, it seems, must be utterly simple. It is prior to all experience, must run through all experience; no empirical cloudiness or uncertainty can be allowed to affect it —It must rather be of the purest crystal. (*PI 97*)

However, without the transcendence discussed here, it can make no sense to talk of *the a priori order of the world*. There will be a whole variety of orders, each articulated from a point of view and for a particular purpose. Once this possibility is exposed, the very distinction between the world as the totality of facts and the world as meant or willed becomes untenable. Even the world-as-the-totality-of-facts is simply a "meant world," and there is no access to what is except by way of different systems of meaning and at the same time no perspective from which to express what "must" be common to these systems of meaning as such. In the context of the *Tractatus* that yields solipsism, but in the context of the *Philosophical Investigations* it only implies a diversity of language games serving a variety of purposes. The limits of a language game are not the a priori limits of all thought or reality; they are the de facto limits of the language serving our purposes here and now.

Ethics and the Project to be God

The problems that are apparent as we think through the relation between the logical and ethical aspects of the *Tractatus* are, of course, also present on each side as well. This should not be surprising by now for, as I have argued, they share a fundamental structure.

By reflecting on the very possibility of the project of the *Tractatus*, we found (in Chapter 4, the section on the unsayable and the metaphysical subject) that its success in putting into words its claims was a violation of those claims. The very existence of that work forces us to treat the metaphysical subject both transcendentally and as an item in the world. At the end of the last chapter we found that Wittgenstein's ethical vision involves a similar self-defeating incoherence. There, however, we only developed that tension in its logical aspects, ending by raising the question of the actual possibility of the ethical life. What I mean is this. Just as the doctrines of the *Tractatus* make it impossible to provide an account of what happens in the work, so also the ethical doctrines make it impossible to provide an account of ethical living. What this means is that as lived, the ethical must either yield an essential frustration or presuppose self-deception. This can be made clear if we ask the question: Why does aesthetic transcendence recommend itself to Wittgenstein as *the* way for the will to achieve its own ethical fulfillment?

A brief review of several aspects of Wittgenstein's view will help to focus an answer. First, there is what was earlier called his Aristotelian strand. For Wittgenstein the "good will" is also and essentially the "happy will." But alongside this Aristotelian insistence that goodness and happiness be conceived in tandem, there is also a Kantian intuition that ethics concerns only what pertains to the will as such. Both elements are combined in the passage quoted earlier from the *Tractatus*.

> When an ethical law of the form, "Thou shalt . . .", is laid down, one's first thought is, "And what if I do not do it?" It is

clear, however, that ethics has nothing to do with punishment and reward in the usual sense of the terms. So our question about the *consequences* of an action must be unimportant.—At least those consequences should not be events. For there must be something right about the question we posed. There must indeed be some kind of ethical reward and ethical punishment, but they must reside in the action itself.

(And it is also clear that the reward must be something pleasant and the punishment something unpleasant.) (*T* 6.422)

Given our previous discussion, it is clear that when Wittgenstein contends that ethical reward must reside in the "action itself," he must mean that ethical reward must reside in the action of the ethical will itself. How and what the will wills must constitute its reward, and this "must be something pleasant." The ethical fulfillment of the will must constitute its happiness, and that happiness, to have ethical value, must concern what pertains to the will as such.

Aesthetic transcendence appears to allow both the Aristotelian and Kantian conditions to be satisfied. The will as an item in the world is at the mercy of the world. Even if a systematic satisfaction of one's desires were "granted by fate," this would have no ethical value since its conditions are beyond the will and so are utterly contingent. This dependence is described in theological terms by Wittgenstein when he says,

we are in a certain sense dependent and what we are dependent on we can call God.

In this sense God would simply be fate, or, what is the same thing: The world—which is independent of our will. (*NB* p. 74, 8.7.16)

Not even God in the sense suggested here can lend ethical significance to a happiness that happens "in the world." Happiness can be

something of *ethical value* only if it does not occur accidentally—
if its conditions are completely within the power of the will. This is
possible only if the will is not an "item in the world" but instead "the
world is *given* to me, i.e. My will enters into the world completely
from outside as something that is already there" (*NB* p. 74, 8.7.16).
The "aesthetic attitude" finally allows the will to achieve an equality
with the world since the will confronts the world as a totality, *sub
specie aeternitatis*. It enters into the world completely from the outside. At the same time, happiness for such a will is an exclusive
function of what the will wills. By taking the world as an aesthetic
object, "I can make myself independent of fate" (*NB* p. 74, 8.7.16).
Only by confronting the world as its co-relative can the will achieve
its true status. But then and paradoxically, "there are two godheads:
the world and my independent I" (*NB* p. 74, 8.7.16). For the traditional God there is no gap between will and fulfillment. Whatever
is, is God's will, and whatever God wills, is. Now, since it must be
the project of the ethical will to be independent of fate—that is, the
world—its project must be to become God. God's power (and my
power) does not consist, however, in bringing about changes "in the
world" but in willing the world itself. To be God is to will the world
and to have that will honored not as an accident or "gift" but in
virtue of the will's having willed it.

This is surely a bold doctrine. The ethical fulfillment of each of
us consists in becoming God. However, as a complete modernist,
Wittgenstein sees, what the Roman Caesars no doubt discovered to
their eternal disappointment, that God can have no role to play in
the world and that nothing in the world can be God! "God does
not reveal himself *in* the world" (*T* 6.432). In the world everything
simply is as it is—there is no room for God's action—there can be
no miracle. "Aesthetically, the miracle is that the world exists. That
what exists does exist" (*NB* p. 86, 20.10.16). The ethical subject as
fulfilled—as God—stands at the limit of the world.

There is a fundamental difference between the traditional God and "my independent I." The traditional God's relation to the world is a metaphysical fact. For the metaphysical theist the world is as God wills it because God's will has infinite power. God creates and sustains the world in its detailed diversity, and so God's will is the ultimate explanatory fact. We have already discussed this position in connection with what Wittgenstein called the "ancient world view." However, we can now see how the metaphysical rendering of God in effect captures the truth and at the same time utterly misconceives it. We might put this by saying that what the metaphysical theist *means* is quite correct; only it cannot be said, but makes itself manifest. (See *T* 5.62.)

The solipsist treats the metaphysical subject as a particular subject when it is merely the totality of facts taken as representable. So the theist treats the will that constitutes the ethical and logical limit of the world as a particular will, which by its willful act *brings into being* the world and by so doing explains its existence. In short, the theist contends that it is a further fact about the world that its existence is a miracle. The contingency of the world must therefore be grounded in the metaphysical fact of God's will. For this will there is no gap between wish and fulfillment because this will is endowed with infinite power, so even creation ex nihilo is possible.

God is not a particular will of infinite power any more than eternal life is life of infinite temporal duration. God is the possibility of willing the world so that will and world coincide. It is this possibility that constitutes the meaning of life and world, which are, after all, the same. So

> To believe in a God means to understand the question about the meaning of life.
>
> To believe in a God means to see that the facts of the world are not the end of the matter.
>
> To believe in God means to see that life has a meaning. (*NB* p. 74, 8.7.16)

While it is clear in light of our discussion that Wittgenstein believed in God, he certainly did not believe in the God of traditional theology. The traditional theologian confuses a formal possibility—*shown* in the presentation of the totality of facts as a totality—with a particular subject.

There can be no individual subject that explains the very existence of the world. Such a God would explicitly violate the Tractarian vision by being both a condition of the world and an item in the world. Where it makes perfect sense to explain particular phenomena, it makes no sense to "explain" the whole, and it is the burden of the *Tractatus* to show this.

Although Wittgenstein's view avoids the pitfalls of traditional theism, there still remains a residue of metaphysics. That there are two god-heads both expresses a truth about the willing subject and at the same time lays down a goal to be achieved. The real nature of the will is expressed in the contention that it has no power over affairs *in the world,* but, of course, this may not be recognized. Most of us most of the time cling to the world in a desperate attempt to have some control *in* the world. But since such attempts can lead only to frustration, it is the ethical purpose of the *Tractatus* to bring about this recognition so that "I can *make* myself independent of fate" and "become a god-head."

It is this dual character that creates the real tension for Wittgenstein. Insofar as we understand the ethical subject as an achievement, it is something that happens to and for a particular individual. The ethical subject is a situated particular subject who "comes to take" a certain attitude to the world. The will that might *become* independent of fate is my will, that is, the will of Michael Hodges. However, the will that *is* independent of fate is not a will at all, any more than the metaphysical subject is a subject. The metaphysical subject is language taken as the possibility of representation so that the limits of what is represented (the facts) coincides with the limits of representing (language). The ethical subject is the possibility of willing so that the object willed (the facts) coincides with the content of the will (the facts as aesthetically appreciated). To "see" the world aright is to "see" the totality of facts as a totality, and to will it aright is to will the totality of facts as the totality-of-facts.

As an achievement, the aesthetic appropriation of the world cannot be something that "happens to" a transcendental subject. Nothing can happen to such a subject. All happenings are numbered among the totality of facts so the will that makes itself independent cannot be that will, but rather it is *my* particular will. But anything that happens in the world—to my particular will—can be of no ethical value. What this means is that insofar as Wittgenstein's ethical ideal is achieved or even achievable, it necessarily loses its *ethical* value, since "in the world everything is as it is, and everything happens as it does happen: *in* it no value exists—and if it did exist, it would have no value" (*T* 6.41).

There are two aspects essential to an understanding of Wittgenstein's position here. On the one hand, there is the demand for absolute value. On the other, there is the recognition that whatever happens in the world is utterly without value. This means that whatever I actually do is without value, but this is experienced against the demand for absolute value. On the one hand, no human project can have any value, and on the other, the will is the demand for value. This establishes for us a project that by its very nature is unachievable. The resulting life can only be one of utter frustration or self-deception.

The demand for absolute value cannot coherently be satisfied. Aesthetic transcendence, if it is achieved by an individual, is simply the attitude of a particular will among others in the world. It cannot claim the sort of uniqueness that Wittgenstein wants. This means that insofar as it is actually achieved, it immediately becomes valueless by reference to the very standard that recommended it. This is true for any and every human project, envisioned or actually realized, and so there is nowhere to rest. Frustration is built into the ethical project as proposed. The frustration could be avoided only by giving up the demand for absolute value. However, within the structure of the *Tractatus* that amounts to the abandonment of ethical value altogether.

If, on the other hand, aesthetic transcendence is constituted by the demand for its own unconditional status, it involves a fundamental self-deception. The self-deception can be seen in the following way. For the ethical subject the choice of anything *in the world* is arbitrary. Everything is of equal value so there can be no reason for choosing one thing or another. Yet the choice of aesthetic transcendence is also a choice *in the world* and is therefore arbitrary, but it treats itself as absolute. The point of view of the ethical subject is constituted by the recognition of the contingency of all human projects as items in the world, but on this view, the ethical subject attempts to avoid this status for itself by claiming to be at the limit of the world. However, this claim cannot be allowed in the sense necessary. Nothing can be both an item in the world and the limit of the world, and this is the overriding lesson of the "refutation of solipsism." Here is the essential duplicity in Wittgenstein's view. The ethical project is the project of taking one conditional human project as unconditional.

Surely for any actual person the attitude of aesthetic transcendence is something that might, at best, be achieved for a moment. It cannot be lived for a whole life. If we really take seriously the de facto nature of our situatedness, the point becomes clear. We are particular beings in the world with particular desires and needs and physical limitations. Our lives, our conscious states, and our well-being are thoroughly dependent on a vast variety of conditions that are not even within our power in "the popular sense." Though it may be possible to ignore or take for granted many of these conditions for a long time, it is simply not possible to sustain such a stance indefinitely. Our very capacity to achieve and sustain aesthetic transcendence is contingent on an actual distribution within the totality of facts.

It might be suggested that we ought, at least, to live our lives in such a way as to maximize the number of occasions on which this transcendence can occur. This, however, does not avoid the criticism. For a particular situated subject, the question "Is aesthetic transcendence possible?" cannot, in principle, be given a final answer. It will be possible so long as the world does not throw up something that disrupts the view of it *sub specie aeternitatis*. But if that is so, then the ability to sustain such an attitude is a "gift of fate" and for that reason cannot be of moral value.

Walker Percy's character Will Barrett in *The Second Coming* offers a clear example.[1] He goes into a cave to await some sign from God, but, unfortunately, he gets a toothache. He is simply overcome by his situatedness. Of course, one might hold that the toothache itself is the sign, but this avenue is not open to Wittgenstein, and in any case it does not escape the problem at hand. First, for Wittgenstein no event in the world can have divine meaning. There simply are no miracles. Second and more importantly, the desire to see such an event as a sign from God is simply the desire for the unconditional project, and it is that notion itself that has been found to be problematic. By rejecting it we do not merely reject the claims of various individual projects to be unconditional; we reject "unconditionality" itself as a standard of willing.

What is true with regard to the ethical subject and the ethical project is also true for the metaphysical subject and the logical project of the *Tractatus*. If the project of aesthetic transcendence is, at best, one among many projects, then by analogy the perspective of the metaphysical subject, from which the totality of facts is a totality, is at best one among many "perspectives." This constitutes the essential turn that separates the early thought from that of the *Investigations*. More will be said about this in the final chapter. Part of the attractiveness of Wittgenstein's ethical vision is clearly tied up with the idea that in some transcendental sense there is a "totality of facts" that I might be co-equal with—a god-head. The illusion of absolute "objectivity" contained in the doctrine of the metaphysical subject prepares the way for the ethical vision. But we have already seen that that doctrine contains its own incoherence. There is no "totality of facts" in the sense that Wittgenstein requires. There are many "totalities," each appearing from the vantage point of a particular "language game." Seen in that light, the very project of the *Tractatus* is the project of taking one particular human mode of language as transcendentally unconditional. In short, the project of the *Tractatus* both ethically and logically is the project to be God, and that project is either conceived in self-deception or can yield nothing but frustration. If absolute transcendence is an illusion, then there is no God, not even in a Tractarian sense, and we are left with only the various projects of situated individuals and/or communities of those individuals, one of which is that of aesthetic appropriation.

The "lived" practical incoherence of the ethical project of the *Tractatus* is paralleled by the intellectual incoherence of its notion of the ethical subject, and both of these are but versions of the very same incoherence we have found in the logical theory itself. This should not be surprising by now. In fact, it is a further confirmation of our whole analysis. We have found the very center of the *Tractatus* around which its problematic seems to turn.

Transcendence Revisited

The problems we have identified can be brought out as follows. (1) Ethics is possible only for a transcendental will. This follows directly from 6.421 and 6.423, where Wittgenstein claims that ethics is transcendental and that the ethical will ("the will in so far as it is the subject of ethical attributes") cannot be spoken about, that is to say, is transcendental. However, (2) the ethical will can be either happy or unhappy. (See *T* 6.43.) (3) For happiness or unhappiness to be ethically relevant, it must depend exclusively on the good or bad exercise of the will (*T* 6.422). But given (1), it follows that (4) "if the good or bad exercise of the will does alter the world, it can alter only the limits of the world, not the facts—not what can be expressed by means of language" (*T* 6.43). And that means that although the world of the happy person is a different world from that of the unhappy person, the difference cannot lie among the facts that are the world (*T* 1.1). Rather, it must be a difference that pertains to the will itself. But (5) any difference between one will and another just is a difference with regard to the facts of the world. Therefore, insofar as happiness or unhappiness is possible for the ethical will, the will cannot be transcendental. However, if the ethical will is not transcendental, ethics is not possible.

There are, at least, two ways to avoid this conclusion. The first focuses on the fifth proposition above. From what point of view is that claim supposed to be true? Of course, if it is a claim about particular empirical wills, it is true, but then its truth would be irrelevant to ethics. As we know, the will as an empirical phenomenon "is of interest only to psychology" (*T* 6.423) and so has no place in our discussion. On the other hand, if it is a claim about the ethical subject, it makes no sense. The ethical subject is transcendental, and there cannot be different transcendental subjects. It would seem that as a statable claim about facts in the world the fifth proposition is irrelevant to ethics, and as relevant to ethics, what it attempts to say cannot be said. Here we have a familiar escape route of Wittgenstein's. The problem is that we have transgressed against the all-important injunction to be silent about matters whereof we cannot speak. The difficulties outlined above arise just because *we* are attempting to put ethics into words. We must simply be silent.

Unfortunately, this will not do, for it is not I but Wittgenstein who has transgressed against his own injunction to be silent. The ethical subject can be unhappy as well as happy, and according to the third proposition above, the difference between the happy and the unhappy person *must* be a difference that pertains to the will.

However, to suppose that there is such a difference implies different wills or different facts concerning a single will. Neither option is acceptable for Wittgenstein since, as we have seen, both require that we treat the ethical subject as an item in the world and so as an empirical will. Rejecting (5) only makes it impossible to account for an essential aspect of Wittgenstein's ethical stance.

Perhaps the problem is with the second proposition in any case. That proposition asserts that both happiness and unhappiness are possible for the ethical subject qua transcendental will. Suppose we reject that. Although this seems to run directly counter to a number of statements in the *Tractatus* and the *Notebooks*, it may be possible to make sense of it in the total context of Wittgenstein's early work. Perhaps we should hold that for a transcendental will only happiness is possible. Unhappiness would then be evidence of the will's failure to achieve transcendence. If one is unhappy with the world, then either there is some fact in the world that cannot be "gotten over" or it is the will's own attitude to the world taken as a whole that is the problem. In either case, the will in question is merely empirical.

This view offers a direct interpretation of the difference between the world of the happy and unhappy person. "The world of the unhappy man," the world from within, is a sphere of action, desire, and purpose where, as we have seen, frustration is unavoidable. The "world of the happy man" is the totality of facts taken from without, from which perspective only acceptance and aesthetic appreciation are possible. This would explain what Wittgenstein means by saying that the good or bad exercise of the will affects only the *limits* of the world. The ethically good exercise of the will wills the world as a limited whole—as a given totality. On the other hand, the bad exercise of the will takes the world not as a completed totality but as an ongoing field of action.

Now, there are not two distinct ethical subjects or even distinct facts about a single subject. There is only a multitude of empirical wills caught up in the affairs of the world and the ethical subject, which is also the happy subject. Transcendence and happiness are co-extensive, for happiness consists in willing the world in such a way that what is willed and what is are necessarily identical. So the ethical subject "shrinks to a point without extension and there remains the reality coordinate with it" (T 5.64). Unhappiness will always involve the failure of the will to "shrink to a point" so that it continues to exist as an item that stands in some potential or actual conflict with the rest of the world.

There are a number of issues raised by this reading. First, note that there seems to be an important asymmetry between the good and bad exercise of will. The unhappy will is, on this view, merely the empirical will. But I argued earlier that both happiness and unhappiness as empirical phenomena are ethically irrelevant. How then can the empirical will be identified with the bad (ethical) exercise of the will? In fact, in various places Wittgenstein seems to reject this line. Consider, for example,

the willing subject would have to be happy or unhappy, and happiness and unhappiness could not be part of the world.

and

As the subject is not a part of the world but a presupposition of its existence, so good and evil are predicates of the subject, not properties in the world. (NB p. 79, 2.8.16)

Both passages locate good and evil, happiness and unhappiness, in a subject that "is not part of the world" and that seems to run counter to the view now being discussed.

Perhaps there is a way to avoid this objection. It is certainly true that the empirical will taken on its own terms is ethically irrelevant. As such, its happiness or unhappiness is ethically irrelevant. However, when empirical willing is seen from the point of view of the ethical subject as transcendental will, all such willing–whether it yields empirical happiness or unhappiness—is, ethically, bad willing. It is ethically bad because, when it is self-consciously seen from the point of view of the ethical subject, it no longer qualifies as what I called "naive prudence" earlier. Rather, it involves a self-conscious commitment to the life of action and purpose in the world. Such a commitment is, of course, the essence of unhappiness for the ethical subject. So, even on the view we are considering, "good and evil only enter through the *subject*" (NB p. 79, 2.8.16), where that subject is the ethical, transcendental will.

Although this reading may make the present interpretation consistent with the text, it does not salvage Wittgenstein's ethical position simply because it does not involve a rejection of the second proposition—both happiness and unhappiness are possible for the ethical will. In order to avoid one problem, we have been forced to reintroduce two distinct "attitudes" of the transcendental ethical will, one that appreciates the world as an aesthetic totality and another that self-consciously commits to a life of action and purpose. The first of these is the happy will, and the second, the unhappy.

Even supposing that we could find a way to avoid the problems here, a far deeper difficulty stands in the way of the current interpretation. In what sense does the happy, ethical will disappear? When we say that by achieving aesthetic transcendence the ethical subject disappears, this means that the ethical subject "disappears" as an *independent* will. That is, there will be nothing willed that is not already in the world. So the content of the will and the world is necessarily the same. But, strictly speaking, the will has not disappeared, for there is an important difference between the world considered merely as the totality of facts and as the *aesthetically appreciated* totality of facts. It is a difference that characterizes the totality. In Wittgenstein's phrase, the world "waxes and wanes as a whole" (T 6.43). As appreciated, the world attains a "glow." The best that I can do to "describe" this is to use the metaphor of a tint that everything takes on. Nothing changes and yet everything comes to have a "tint of appreciation" like a rosey glow! It is just this difference that Wittgenstein has in mind when he says, "If I am right, then it is not sufficient for the ethical judgment that a world is given" (*NB* p. 79, 2.8.16). The point is that unless the will exists, even though it is transparent as to content, the whole notion of happiness loses all sense.

If there is literally no will, then there is simply nothing to be happy. Such a literal disappearance of the will may be what Wittgenstein has in mind when he says, "At death the world does not alter, but comes to an end" (*T* 6.431). If there were no will, there would be no ethical world. But happiness is not death. And this means that insofar as happiness is attained, the way the ethical subject wills the world is another fact within the world. The totality of facts includes the fact that I aesthetically appreciate that totality. As such, attained happiness loses its standing as ethical.

Every attempt to make out what Wittgenstein has in mind seems to draw the ethical subject back into the world and thus make ethics impossible. We seem to be confronted by a puzzle. If ethics can be "talked about," it cannot be ethics. To talk about the ethical subject necessarily locates it in the world. Perhaps what should be done is merely to "Live Happily!" (*NB* p. 75, 8.7.16) and be silent. And so again we confront the showing/saying distinction. However, the issues that surround that complex topic can be put in the following form at this point. If the *Tractatus* is to have any philosophical role, there must be two different sorts of silence. There is the silence of the boor (to borrow William James's example from "The Sentiment of Rationality"[2]), and there is the silence of the savant who has been led to see what the *Tractatus* is supposed to show us. For the boor, the problem of the meaning of life does not arise because it has simply never occurred to him or her to raise any questions. Nothing is problematic only because the boor has never given anything any thought. On the other hand, the silence of the savant is a silence won through long and complex reflection. It is an informed silence. But, of course, strictly taken, the silence of the savant cannot be distinguished from that of the boor because the former cannot give an account of itself. Any attempt to give such an account leads back to the problem of what it is that the *Tractatus* itself is supposed to do and how it does it.

At the very end of the *Tractatus*, Wittgenstein seems to pull the rug out from under his own feet when he says,

> My propositions serve as elucidations in the following way: anyone who understands me eventually recognizes them as nonsensical, when he has used them—as steps—to climb up beyond them. (He must, so to speak, throw away the ladder after he has climbed up it.) (*T* 6.54)

Surely the key to any possible interpretation here depends on paying particular attention to Wittgenstein's contrast between understanding *him* and understanding the propositions of the *Tractatus*. Since by its own account the propositions of the *Tractatus* are "nonsensical," understanding them cannot be a matter of coming to see what they say, for they say nothing. So understanding Wittgenstein is a matter of recognizing that his propositions are nonsensical. Perhaps the sentences contained in the text *cause* a change of the appropriate kind. On this view, reading the *Tractatus* could be seen as part of a discipline the end result of which is a certain change in thinking. But surely this will not do because such a claim could be understood only as a prediction and would, therefore, be false for a large range of cases since no such change may be forthcoming (and is, generally, not forthcoming, if we go by the general readership). More importantly, however, any causal result of reading would itself be an item in the world and so would lead us right back into the difficulties discussed above.

There is a further possibility to consider. Suppose that the *Trac-*

tatus really makes no positive claims at all. Suppose that the correct way to conceive it is as a reductio ad absurdum. The transcendence of the work is to be understood as a hypothetical starting point that, when rigorously developed, leads to its own impossibility. The attempt to think from a transcendental point of view is shown to be self-defeating so that we are finally brought to see the futility of the project itself. In this way we see that "the solution to the problem of life is seen in the vanishing of the problem" (*T* 6.521).

As an account of the *Tractatus*, this is not satisfactory. As we have seen, "the problem of life" vanishes by achieving aesthetic transcendence, not by recognizing the impossibility of transcendence. If we accept this view, what are we to make of the whole positive account of ethical achievement as aesthetic appreciation, developed earlier? Remember Paul Englemann's point that for Wittgenstein the task of delimiting what can be said was done, not for the sake of what falls within that domain but for the sake of what does not. Englemann contends that Wittgenstein has much to be silent about, but on this view there is nothing to be silent about. On this negative view, the *Tractatus* would simply be equivalent to some form of positivism, so none of the ethical vision developed in it or in the *Notebooks* has any standing. In any case, positivism traditionally conceived faces the same problem we are discussing here. All standard forms of that view seem to require the same sort of exemption for their own claims that the *Tractatus* does. That is, positivism in stating its own principle of meaningfulness violates that principle.

There is finally no escape from the difficulties present in the ethical dimensions of the *Tractatus*. And as we have seen, these problems are not limited to the ethical aspects of Wittgenstein's early philosophy. They have analogues on the logical side as well. Although the reductio account will not do as a positive interpretation of the *Tractatus*, it may hold the key to Wittgenstein's understanding of that work in his later period. In the final analysis only a negative lesson can be coherently taken away from the *Tractatus*, and it is just this negative lesson that opens the door to the later philosophy and shows us how it is possible to reject the transcendence of the *Tractatus* and at the same time avoid positivism. There is, of course, a real question left in all this. What sort of ethical vision goes along with the later philosophy? The answer, perhaps, lies in the direction of a kind of acceptance not structured by transcendence and with it the demand for absolute value.[3]

8

CONCLUSION

For both the logical and ethical dimensions of Wittgenstein's early thought, there is an unavoidable internal tension. It manifests itself on the logical side in the attempt to "say"—the saying that is the *Tractatus*—what, according to the *Tractatus*, cannot be said. On the ethical side it manifests itself in the demand for absolute value that makes its actual achievement incoherent.

These are but two symptoms of a single philosophical disease— the attempt to think from a "transcendental point of view." The very project of the *Tractatus* is statable only from such a vantage point. Only from a perspective beyond both language and the world can the problem of language, as the *Tractatus* formulates it, be a problem, and only from that perspective can its solution be "articulated." However, as our discussion so clearly shows, such a perspective always fails to take account of itself. This is perhaps most obvious in the *Tractatus* on the ethical side, where we are forced to treat the ethical subject both as transcendental and as one among others. However, as we have seen, the problem is not limited to Wittgenstein's ethical insights. If the perspective of the metaphysical subject is necessarily the perspective of the *Tractatus* itself, then what the *Tractatus* attempts to say cannot be said, and we are condemned to a silence that can give no account of itself. On the other hand, if that perspective is accessible, then, by the very standards of the *Tractatus*, it is one among others, and any claims made from that perspective cannot be construed as setting the a priori, *absolute* limits to all possible language.

The problem that Wittgenstein confronts here is by no means unique to him, although with him it has, perhaps, its purest form. It takes its original shape at the very beginning of modern philosophy in the Cartesian project to *think* through the relation between thought and reality, having drawn a radical distinction between the two. Descartes quickly saw that, once the order of thought is separated from the order of things, nothing that could be thought could guarantee a relation between the two. Each new thought simply raises the same question again. Similarly, Locke began with access only to ideas and their structure in radical juxtaposition to the world and its structure and then attempted to account for the relation between ideas and the world. So Wittgenstein begins with language and its structure in the same relation to the world. But if we do begin with the dichotomy between language and the world and bind ourselves up on the side of language, it becomes impossible to state how meaningful language is possible. The only solution to such a problem would be a deus ex machina, as Descartes clearly saw. In effect, only a thought beyond all thought would do. Now, although the early Wittgenstein holds out no hope for divine intervention, he is committed to a language that is beyond all language—the language of the *Tractatus* itself—and that only shows that the problem as formulated cannot be solved. What is needed is a reexamination and finally a rejection of the beginning point that gives rise to it in the first place.

What creates the problem for Locke, Descartes, and the early Wittgenstein is the radical and in principle gulf between the order of thought or language and the order of things, which can "appear" only if the subject can somehow stand off from both. This gulf is formulatable only in a language that itself takes both language and world as its subject matter. But such a language is essentially "beyond language." It is the language of the *Tractatus*. The picture is of a language that is essentially beyond the world and that must, from that perspective, represent it. As we have seen, this is nowhere more clearly stated than in Wittgenstein's discussion of the philosophical self in the *Tractatus*: "The philosophical self is not the human being, not the human body, not the human soul, with which psychology deals, but rather the metaphysical subject, the limit of the world—not a part of it" (*T* 5.641). Just as Descartes's problem requires for its solution a subject—God—that is beyond all subjects, so Wittgenstein's problem requires for its "solution" a subject—the metaphysical subject—that is beyond all subjects.

There are and must be two selves in the *Tractatus*. There is the one described in language, and there is one that authors the book *The World as I found it*, but that is not and cannot be described therein. (See *T* 5.631.) Of course, that book just is the *Tractatus*. So there are two "languages." On the one hand, there is the language that is the explicit subject matter of the work. That is the language that pictures facts, the limits of which are also the limits of the world. But there is also the language in which the first language is described. That is the language of the *Tractatus*, and that language does not and cannot satisfy the conditions for meaningfulness that it lays down for language. The essential problem can be put as follows. Unless there are these two languages, the *Tractatus* cannot be written, for language in the first sense is incapable of expressing what the *Tractatus* expresses. Without the two languages there would be only a silence that can give no account of itself. But if there are two languages, then what the *Tractatus* "says" about language must be false. So if the *Tractatus* succeeds in saying what it purports to say, that very success denies what is said. If, on the other hand, what is said is true, then the *Tractatus* is meaningless. The *Tractatus* (which is the saying of that truth) must, therefore, be, at one and the same time, meaningful (to be true or false) and meaningless by its own standards of meaning. That is what is meant by saying that the *Tractatus* cannot take account of itself.

If we are to reconceive the project of the *Tractatus*, all this must be rejected. Language must be viewed as already embedded in the world, already serving human purposes. These purposes will not be the purposes of a transcendental subject, but the more mundane purposes of human beings. For the later philosophy the "metaphysical subject" *is* the human being or, rather, the community of human language users. Language has a place in the activities of human beings —in their activities as builders and grocers, for example. Thus the *later* Wittgenstein constantly asks us to focus on the activities, facts, and purposes that surround the use of language, not because these are somehow "represented" in the language but because it is by reference to them that we are to show how language is possible. In fact, the monolithic notion of language is replaced with that of "language game." These linguistic activities are introduced as limited wholes situated in relation to other language games and in relation to a background of activities, both linguistic and nonlinguistic.

The earliest examples of language games that Wittgenstein calls to our attention already involve the use of sounds and written marks *in the context of various sorts of activities*. The language game of Wittgenstein's builders (*PI* 2) is developed against a background of activities—not only of building but also of training. He says,

> We could imagine that the language of 2 was the *whole* language of A and B; even the whole language of a tribe. The children are brought up to perform *these* activities, to use *these* words as they do and to react in *this* way to the words of others. (*PI* 6)

It is essential to an understanding of this language game that we view it in the context of the activities that surround it and so make it possible. We must be aware of the ways in which children actually learn to use it—what methods of training work and how language users relate in different contexts and situations. Wittgenstein's stress on "these activities," "these words," and "this way" is meant to focus us on the concrete particularities of the situation of use and learning. There can be no pretense to "giving an account of language as such" if for no other reason than that no such thing as language as such can appear if we take account of our own situatedness—if we attend to the particularities of the situation of learning and use.

Wittgenstein goes on to say, "I shall also call the whole, consisting of language and the actions into which it is woven, the 'language game'" (*PI* 7). This completely innocent-looking remark is actually the encapsulation of a radically distinctive stance. The point is that language does not and cannot describe the world from a transcendent perspective. Language games are as much a part of the world that they describe as are the things described. "To imagine a language means to imagine a form of life" (*PI* 19). It is impossible to isolate language from the nexus of activities in which it occurs. A language is a language for beings of a certain sort—beings that share a common base of interests and activities, or what Wittgenstein here calls a "form of life." Thus, to imagine a language is to imagine such speakers of the language and to imagine the life they live.

The apparent metaphysical question of the *Tractatus*, "How is language related to the world?" is to be answered not by providing a mystical view of an unspeakable relation. Rather, it is to be answered in a much more mundane and certainly philosophically unsatisfying way—by showing how, in a multitude of different ways, language games relate to the various sorts of activities that we, language users, perform, including even the activity of using language itself. In this, the Tractarian picture of language as beyond the world has been replaced by a view of language in the world. Of course, this is also extended to the subject, which is no longer a pure subject beyond the world but an active agent in the world which that activity takes for granted. In this sense, language and thought presuppose a world and already occur within it.

Wittgenstein develops this point when he says, "The truth of certain empirical propositions belongs to our frame of reference" (OC 83). Truths about the sorts of creatures we are, the sorts of purposes we have, and even the kind of world we live in create the context in which questions of meaning, evidence, and truth arise. Our frame of reference, or what he calls elsewhere our "picture of the world," is an "inherited background" against which we distinguish the true and the false (OC 94). Our "frame of reference" plays a dual role here. On the one hand, it is the background against which we distinguish the true and the false. From a Tractarian point of view, that role would require that it be prior to truth and falsity, as objects, for example, are prior to facts. But Wittgenstein also says that the *truth* of certain empirical statements belongs to that frame of reference. In this way the frame cannot be prior to truth at all. These two passages taken together affirm the impossibility of a Tractarian transcendental or "external" approach to language. Obviously, if there being empirical truths presupposes the meaningfulness of the language in which they are stated and at the same time the meaningfulness of that language presupposes the truths, the project of the *Tractatus*, to present the a priori limits to all possible language, cannot even be envisioned since the notion of the "a priori" presupposed by the project is no longer available.

A clear example of this interrelation of truth and meaning is found in Part II of the *Philosophical Investigations*. Wittgenstein says,

> Does it make sense to say that people generally agree in their judgments of colour? What would it be like for them not to? —One man would say a flower was red which another called blue, and so on.—But what right should we have to call these people's words "red" and "blue" *our* 'colour-words'?—
>
> How would they learn to use these words? And is the language-game which they learn still such as we call the use of 'names of colour'? There are evidently differences of degree here. (*PI* II, p. 226)

Clearly, we are to be puzzled about how to answer the question. The initial temptation is to suppose that the answer is nonproblematical. Isn't it obvious that people agree? But given the discourse of "judgments of colour," it cannot be a mere matter of fact that people generally agree. For the mark "blue" to be a color word, it *must* be the case that there is general agreement in its use. Were there no such agreement, that mark and the others which, as things stand, are in the same family would not play the role they do for us—they would not be color words. The problem with the question is that it invites us to think in terms of two independent elements—judgments of color and agreement in the use of color terms. In short, it invites us to treat meaning as given prior to the facts that surround usage. It invites us to think in Tractarian terms.

The assertion that people generally agree in their judgments is in a sense "tautological," for its denial is self-defeating, if not self-contradictory. Without the relevant agreement, the words in question would not be color words. This interdependence is clearly stated at *PI* 242:

> If language is to be a means of communication there must be agreement not only in definitions but also (queer as this may sound) in judgments. This seems to abolish logic, but does not do so.—It is one thing to describe methods of measurement, and another to obtain and state results of measurement. But what we call "measuring" is partly determined by a certain constancy in results of measurement.

For there to be a practice of the sort that is "making judgments of colour," those who participate in the practice must make roughly the same judgments. If that were not so, and it is perfectly possible that it might not be, whatever might be happening would not count as "making colour judgments." The agreement in question is a presupposition of there being color judgments so that the denial of the original claim is nonsense. But, of course, "there are evidently differences of degree here."

This agreement is not a "transcendental condition" of the possibility of color judgments. This is shown by the recognition that it is perfectly possible that we might not be the sorts of creatures for which the practice of making color judgments exists. There is nothing necessary about that, but even that formulation has an air of absurdity about it since to say what sorts of creatures we might not be requires that we know what the practice of making color judgments (which might not exist) is. Our attempts to speak intelligibly here seem to run aground by presupposing what they call into question. The way of raising the question—by specifying the situation in terms of color words—is inconsistent with the possibility we are asked to consider in relation to the situation so specified. But it is, of course, possible that where there is agreement now, there might be no agreement. Wittgenstein finally drives the point home when he says,

> I am not saying: if such-and-such facts of nature were different people would have different concepts (in the sense of an hypothesis). But: if anyone believes that certain concepts are absolutely the correct ones, and that having different ones would mean not realizing something that we realize—then let him imagine certain very general facts of nature to be different from what we are used to, and the formation of concepts different from the usual ones will become intelligible to him. (*PI* II, p. 230)

So, it is just a fact about our community of language users that we agree in certain ways, and that fact does make the language game of color judgment possible. The words mean what they do because as a matter of fact human beings are alike in this specifiable way. Being alike in these and other ways is a matter of sharing a common "form of life." That is why Wittgenstein introduces the passage dealing with color judgments by saying, "What has to be accepted, the given, is—so one could say—*forms of life*" (*PI* II, p. 226). And with regard to a different example he says,

> "So you are saying that human agreement decides what is true and what is false?"—It is what human beings *say* that is true and false; and they agree in the *language* they use. This is not agreement in opinions but in form of life. (*PI* 241–242)

Underlying the very possibility of having a common language and therefore opinions about which we can disagree at all are various complex ways in which we are alike.

The difference between the Wittgenstein of the *Tractatus* and that of the *Philosophical Investigations* is focused in a particularly clear way by comparing the sections we have been examining and 2.0211 of the *Tractatus*. There he says that it cannot be the case that whether one proposition has sense depends on the truth of another for "in that case we could not sketch out any picture of the world (true or false)" (*T* 2.0212). In the *Tractatus*, to be a proposition, true or false, is to be a picture of a possible fact. Therefore, whatever is presupposed in being a picture must be prior to all questions of truth or falsity. Only if a set of marks is a picture does it make sense to ask whether it is accurate or correct.

If *A*'s having sense depended on the truth of *B*, then if *B* were false, *A* would be meaningless. So if *A* had figured in our "sketch" of the world, that sketch would be meaningless. And since once we allow the possibility of such interdependence, it cannot be ruled out a priori, we would have no place to begin. Before we could determine the meaningfulness of one proposition, we would have to determine the truth of another, which would require a prior determination of the meaningfulness of that proposition and with it the truth and so meaningfulness of another, and so on. We would have built a house of cards. At some point, meaning must be prior, absolutely prior, to truth. This is the vision of the *Tractatus*. Now, since the project of the *Tractatus* is to say what is necessary for any and every meaningful assertion, it follows that those conditions, whatever they might be, cannot be numbered among the possible truths. Thus, it cannot be true or false, for example, that there are objects. This "shows" itself by there being meaningful language at all.

Now, if we take seriously the interdependence of meaning and truth developed in the later philosophy, we can "construct an argument" that runs contrary to that just stated. If the meaning of one proposition does depend on the truth of another, then meaning will not be given prior to truth. So it will be impossible to specify the a priori limits of language. It will be impossible even to express the project of the *Tractatus* just because it will be impossible to set before ourselves the "totality of language." There is no such totality, since any "totality" will depend for its specification on "the truth of certain empirical propositions" that are part of "our frame of reference," (OC 83). The very idea of a Tractarian totality is incoherent. But if such a totality cannot be specified, there will be no way to "set its limits."

So for the later Wittgenstein, any "theory of language" must presuppose facts about ourselves and our place in the world. No one or any set of these facts, however, is immune from inquiry but, at the same time, each inquiry must have a beginning and an end.

> All testing, all confirmation and disconfirmation of a hypothesis takes place already within a system. And this system is not a more or less arbitrary and doubtful point of departure for all our arguments: no, it belongs to the essence of what we call an argument. The system is not so much the point of departure, as the element in which arguments have their life. (OC 105)

Here, Wittgenstein may seem to be attempting to do the very thing that he denied the possibility of in the *Tractatus*—to describe in language the relation between language and the world. In fact, he is quite aware of this very point. He says,

> Indeed doesn't it seem obvious that the possibility of a language-game is conditioned by certain facts?
>
> In that case it would seem as if the language-game must 'show' the facts that make it possible. (But that's not how it is.) (OC 617–618)

The showing/saying distinction of the *Tractatus* is finally rejected. As we have seen, the problem that required such a distinction has taken on a new form. The task is not to show from without how it is that language maps onto the world, for that task presupposes notions of "world and language" that come into focus only from a transcendental Tractarian point of view. By abandoning the idea of an articulable perspective beyond both language and the world, we also abandon the very notions of "world and language" used to formulate the problem. If the perspective of the *Tractatus* is incoherent, then the ideas of the world as "the totality of facts" and of language as "picturing" that totality are also incoherent. There can be no such perspective. The illusion that there can has been shown by the author of the *Tractatus* to lead directly to philosophical nonsense.

The illusion, however, is not easily put to rest and may lead followers of the later Wittgenstein into similar philosophical nonsense. One may proclaim, contra the *Tractatus*, that language is relative to human interests, purposes, and actions so that the problem of relating thought and the world is solved via a human-centered philosophy that denies the intelligibility of the very notion of objectivity that created the problem in the first place. But the problem that Wittgenstein sees with proposing this sort of view is that it can make no sense to claim that it is true. Either that assertion will transgress its own limits by claiming for itself a status that it asserts no statement can have, or it will beg the question by assuming its own truth. If it is true, then there cannot be any nonperspectival truths, and so it cannot be such a truth. But, then, what is the point of asserting it? As a mere perspectival claim it seems to have no philosophical status. On the other hand, if we suppose it to be true in a sense where truth is not already understood perspectivally, then we have allowed in allowing that this claim is true in that sense, what we deny by asserting it. In short, it would seem that any theory that would deny the central claim of the *Tractatus* would, by so doing, transcend its own limits. It must say more than can be said. That is, it falls into the trap of the *Tractatus*.

The very desire to assert the "truth" of the human-centered view seems to drive us in the direction of the transcendental ideal. But again, if the claim is that all propositions are perspectivally determined, so, of course, is that one. And then what can be meant by asserting it? The problem is that the very idea of "asserting a claim" here calls forth a Tractarian interpretation. Perhaps this is why Wittgenstein avoids making *any* claims in the *Philosophical Investigations*. Rather, he "assembles reminders" (*PI* 127) to show that a certain ideal is empty—the ideal that I have referred to throughout as the "transcendental perspective." Implicit in that ideal is the demand for complete "objectivity" or, failing that, a completely objective denial of the possibility of attaining such an ideal. In either case, we must break free of all perspectives for a moment to see the "truth." Having done so, we are immediately dragged down into the mire of mere perspective again. It is this "mystical" breaking free that the author of the *Tractatus* thought he had accomplished. However, the author of the *Philosophical Investigations* cannot accept that. It is not that he rejects the mystical, but rather that he rejects the mystical as the ultimate ground for the intelligibility of language.

We are under the illusion that what is peculiar, profound, essential, in our investigations, resides in its trying to grasp the incomparable essence of language. That is, the order existing between the concepts proposition, word, proof, truth, experience,

and so on. This order is a *super* order between—so to speak
—*super*-concepts. Whereas of course, if the words "language",
"experience", "world", have a use, it must be as humble a one
as that of the words "table", "lamp", "door." (*PI* 97)

We must rid ourselves of the notion that language is a mystical thing
that requires a mystical ground. It is not and it does not. Rather, it
is a natural phenomenon that must be studied and understood in its
own habitat—the world of human beings and human activities.

It is interesting to notice how close to the truth Wittgenstein was
at the end of the *Tractatus*. If what we have said is correct, then
the proper method of philosophy will not be to propose thesis and
counterthesis, for each will be equally one-sided and infected with
the seeds of nonsense.

> The correct method in philosophy would really be the follow-
> ing: to say nothing except what can be said . . . i.e., something
> that has nothing to do with philosophy—and then, whenever
> someone else wants to say something metaphysical, to demon-
> strate to him that he had failed to give meaning to certain signs
> in his propositions. . . . *This* method would be the only strictly
> correct one. (*T* 6.53)

This, of course, is the method of the *Philosophical Investigations*,
and if what we have said is true, it is the only method consistent
with the rejection of the problem of the *Tractatus*.

NOTES

Chapter 1

1. A. J. Ayer, *Language, Truth, and Logic* (New York: Dover Publications, 1952).

2. A. Janik and S. Toulmin, *Wittgenstein's Vienna* (New York: Simon and Schuster, 1973), p. 20.

3. As printed in G. H. von Wright's *Wittgenstein* (Minneapolis: University of Minnesota Press, 1982), p. 83.

4. P. M. S. Hacker, *Insight and Illusion* (New York: Oxford University Press, 1975), p. 83.

5. Janik and Toulmin, *Wittgenstein's Vienna*, p. 16.

6. Ibid., p. 168.

7. S. Kierkegaard, *Fear and Trembling*, trans. by W. Lowrie (Princeton, N.J.: Princeton University Press, 1954).

8. Because of the nature of this work—it is a collection of comments over thirty-seven years, during which Wittgenstein's ideas were changing radically—it is dangerous to quote anything in support of particular claims without careful attention to the date and context. However, the passage here presented is representative of many that express Wittgenstein's attitude, including some from the *Tractatus* itself and the "Lecture on Ethics."

9. Janik and Toulmin, *Wittgenstein's Vienna*, p. 99.

10. Ibid., p. 48.

11. Ibid., p. 197.

12. E. Bullough, " 'Psychical Distance' as a Factor in Art and an Aesthetic Principle," *British Journal of Psychology* 5 (1912): 87–98. As reprinted in *Problems in Aesthetics*, ed. by M. Weitz, 2nd ed. (New York: Macmillan, 1970), pp. 782–92.

13. B. Russell, "A Free Man's Worship" in *Mysticism and Logic* (New York: W. W. Norton, 1929), pp. 46–58.

14. G. E. Moore, *Principia Ethica* (Cambridge: Cambridge University Press, 1903).

15. That Wittgenstein was familiar with *Principia Ethica* is clear from various sources, including a reference to it at the beginning of his "Lecture on Ethics" and a letter to Russell in 1912, as quoted in B. F. McGuinness, *Wittgenstein: A Life* (Berkeley: University of California Press, 1988), p. 109.

16. Moore, *Principia Ethica*, p. 188.

17. Ibid., p. 189.

18. Wittgenstein said of *Principia Ethica*, "I do not like it at all" (letter to Russell in 1912, quoted in *Wittgenstein: A Life*, p. 109), but that is not inconsistent with the point I am making here. See the discussion of Russell's influence, below, for an explanation.

19. V. Woolf, *To the Lighthouse* (New York: Harcourt Brace, 1927).

20. As quoted in S. P. Rosenbaum, ed., *The Bloomsbury Group* (Toronto: University of Toronto Press, 1975), p. 52.

21. See Alasdair MacIntyre's *After Virtue* (Notre Dame, Ind.: University of Notre Dame Press, 1981), p. 14.

22. Ibid., p. 15.

23. Bullough, " 'Psychical Distance,' " p. 783.

24. Ibid., p. 782.

25. Ibid., p. 783.

26. Ibid.

27. Wittgenstein was certainly familiar with these materials. See McGuinness, *Wittgenstein: A Life*, pp. 107–9.

28. Russell, "A Free Man's Worship," pp. 55–56.

29. From Russell's "The Essence of Religion" as quoted in *Wittgenstein: A Life*, p. 108.

30. *Wittgenstein: A Life*, p. 108.

31. Aesthetic contemplation requires the very notion of distance as disinterestedness that is mentioned here. See the previous discussion of Bullough.

32. Von Wright, *Wittgenstein*, p. 83.

33. Something Russell had argued for in the final chapter of *The Problem of Philosophy* and a discussion Wittgenstein found utterly problematic.

34. See the Preface of the *Tractatus* (p. 3) where Wittgenstein says that his thoughts can be grasped only by someone who has already had them.

35. Here, of course, the characteristic ideas of the *Philosophical Investigations* come clearly into focus. See particularly pp. 1–7 and 23.

Chapter 3

1. See M. Black, *A Companion to Wittgenstein's Tractatus* (Ithaca, N.Y.: Cornell University Press, 1964), pp. 376–86.
2. Ibid., p. 381.
3. Ibid., p. 382.
4. Ibid.

Chapter 4

1. See Russell's introduction to the *Tractatus*; Hintikka's article in I. Copi and R. W. Beard, *Essays on Wittgenstein's Tractatus* (London: Routledge and Kegan Paul, 1966); C. Lewy "A Note on the Text of the *Tractatus*," *Mind*, vol. 76, 1967. David Pears points out that Wittgenstein, himself, endorsed this translation. See D. Pears, *The False Promise* (Oxford: Clarendon Press, 1987), p. 173.

Chapter 5

1. As I noted in Chapter 1, Wittgenstein said in a letter to von Ficker concerning the publication of the *Tractatus*, "the book's point is an ethical one."
2. M. Black, *A Companion to Wittgenstein's Tractatus* (Ithaca, N.Y.: Cornell University Press, 1964), p. 365.

Chapter 6

1. See Epictetus, *Enchiridion*, trans. by T. W. Higginson (New York: Library of Liberal Arts, 1948), pp. 18–19.
2. S. Kierkegaard, *Fear and Trembling*, trans. by W. Lowrie (Princeton, N.J.: Princeton University Press, 1954), p. 38.
3. On this point see Bullough's essay, discussed briefly in Chapter 1.

Chapter 7

1. W. Percy, *The Second Coming* (New York: Farrar, Straus, Giroux, 1980).

2. W. James, "The Sentiment of Rationality," in *Essays in Pragmaticism* (New York: Hafner Press, 1948), p. 10.

3. For development of some of these ideas in the context of the later philosophy of Wittgenstein, see J. Edwards, *Ethics without Philosophy* (Tampa: University Presses of Florida, 1982).

INDEX